LAMPORT & HOLT LINE
by
Paul Heaton

P.M. Heaton Publishing
Abergavenny Monmouthshire
Great Britain
2004

Front cover: the liner *Vauban* of 1912 from a watercolour by Laurence Dunn.

Back cover: The turbine steamer *Romney* (2) of 1952 shown in the English Channel, and the containership *Churchill* which entered Lamport & Holt Line service in 1986.   *(Fotoflite incorporating Skyfotos)*

Title page: The passenger liner *Vandyck* (3) built by Workman, Clark & Co. Ltd., Belfast in 1921 for the New York, Brazil and River Plate trade. She is seen in her cruising livery post 1932.   *(Stewart Bale Ltd.)*

Page 4: A trials photograph in 1940 of the *Debrett*.   *(Harland & Wolff Ltd., Belfast)*

Dedicated to Lamport's Old & Bold

ISBN 1 872006 16 7

© First Edition October, 2004
P.M. Heaton

Published by P.M. Heaton Publishing
Abergavenny, Monmouthshire, NP7 8NG

Printed in Great Britain by
The Amadeus Press Ltd.,
Cleckheaton, West Yorkshire, BD19 4TQ

Typesetting and page layout by
Highlight Type Bureau Ltd., Bradford BD8 7BY

CONTENTS

PREFACE

I have been a student of the history of Liverpool's Lamport & Holt Line since my youth. Admiring their ships moored in South Wales ports when I was at school. Serving on their vessels *Chatham, Constable* and *Romney* usually in the Brazil and River Plate trades in the early 1960s, and have compiled the history of this famous company twice before. In 1977 my researches were produced in the magazine *Sea Breezes* and in 1986 I published the volume *Lamport & Holt*. On these two occasions the work was heralded with news of developments in the company. In 1977 the news that four S.D. 14 cargo ships had been ordered for the trade to Brazil & the River Plate, and in 1986 that the container ship *Churchill* alone was maintaining their service. Alas, on this my third work, it follows the disappearance of this old established company after almost 150 years in existence.

Whilst I am no academic, it is fitting that this work is compiled by someone who served with them. I am fascinated by Lamport & Holt's history – such a business which had so much to do with the development of the trades to South America from the United Kingdom, Antwerp and New York, and operated a fleet of upwards of fifty ships. Early mail contracts were regularly maintained, the majority of the United States' coffee requirements were carried in their ships and passenger liners were all features of their history. All this after operating sailing ships worldwide and a heavy involvement in the Alexandria trade bringing cotton homewards for Lancashire's mills. This was a company whose men and ships had served during two World Wars, but was involved in service to the country way back in the Crimean War and the Boer War.

My introduction and acknowledgements to the 1986 volume are reproduced in full. I have drawn heavily on unpublished personal accounts by former personnel which was not fully utilised previously. I am also appreciative of Duncan Haws work *Merchant Fleets – Lamport & Holt and Booth* (1998) and the book *Saint John Ships and Their Builders* by Esther Clark Wright (1975) which give a wider view of Lamport & Holt's involvement in sailing ships than I had hitherto known.

To all who have helped – thank you.

Paul Heaton
Abergavenny
October, 2004

INTRODUCTION

During one of my many visits to Newport Docks in my youth I saw an unusual motorship, the *Debrett*, which had part of her accommodation and the bridge incorporated into the funnel. I was impressed by her sheer workmanlike appearance and her recently painted and well maintained hull. Her funnel colours, blue with a black top divided by a white band were outstanding by their simplicity. Such was my interest that I established that she was owned by the Liverpool based shipping company, the Lamport and Holt Line, which operated services from the United Kingdom, Continent and New York to and from Brazil and the River Plate, and was in fact loading cargo for the latter region. In 1960 I was fortunate enough to be invited aboard this company's flagship, the turbine steamer *Romney* which was lying at Swansea, and again was impressed by the high standards to which the ship was maintained.

Further enquiries revealed that the Lamport and Holt Line was, like the Blue Star Line and the Booth Steamship Company, a part of the Vestey Group of companies. This was an organisation with which my grandfather had been employed before the Second World War at their meat processing plant, the Anglo Frigorifico at Dock Sud, Buenos Aires in the post of analytical chemist. Therefore, when in 1961, I decided to go to sea at the comparatively young age of sixteen years, it was little wonder that I should choose the Lamport and Holt Line, and be fortunate enough to be accepted as a Deck Cadet. At that time the company owned in excess of twenty ships and chartered in many more as and when required in order to maintain their services. In the following two and half years I sailed in their vessels, *Chatham, Constable* and *Romney*, and worked-by on the *Rossetti* and *Dryden* at Liverpool.

Some decade or so later I started to take an interest in maritime history, and spent a number of years studying the history of this famous company. The Lamport and Holt Line had been established in 1845 when William James Lamport and George Holt had entered into partnership, and has had a continuous existence as shipowners to the present day. The result of my researches appeared in the shipping magazine *Sea Breezes* from June to December 1977, but since then a number of further developments have taken place, and as a result I decided to write this expanded volume devoted to the company's history.

I have started with an account of the founders' origins, followed by details of the various developments in the Lamport and Holt Line's history up to the present day when the container ship *Churchill* maintains their services. I hope that readers will be as fascinated by the company's history as much as I am, and to former Lamport and Holt personnel I trust they will find that my efforts have been worthwhile.

P.M. Heaton
December 1986

ACKNOWLEDGEMENTS

In compiling this history of the Lamport and Holt Line I would like to acknowledge my appreciation for the wealth of information and assistance freely given by the following:–

To Lamport and Holt Line Ltd., management and staff, current and past, both shorebased and seagoing – Messrs. D.A. Barber, E.V. Atkin, D. Green, R.W. Dutton, A.C. Berry, L. Ross, T. Waring, F. Evans, H. Binney, F.J. Page, M. Roberts and Captains T. Edgar, B.S. Haikney, B.M. Metcalf, D.C. Roberts, G.E. Roberts, H.W. Underhill, S. Dickinson, W.A. Sparks, J.I. Jones, W.A. Wilson and F. Martin.

To others for their assistance, including the World Ship Society Central Record Team, past and present – Messrs. G.H. Somner, H.S. Appleyard, K. O'Donoghue, P.L. White, A.L. Bland, L. Gray and the Rev. D. Ridley Chesterton; Messrs. W.A. Laxon of Auckland, New Zealand; E.K. Haviland of Baltimore, U.S.A.; G. Binns of Sao Paulo, Brazil; J. Lingwood, Sunderland; R.B. Bibby, Southampton; M.J.C. Bamford, Rocester; and to the Moss Hutchinson Line Ltd., Liverpool, Austin & Pickersgill Ltd., Shipbuilders, Sunderland; and the National Maritime Museum, London.

To the following who have kindly provided photographs – Stewart Bale Ltd., Liverpool; A. Duncan, Gravesend; FotoFlite, Ashford; Harland and Wolff Ltd., Belfast; F.W. Hawks, Gillingham; J.A. Macleod, Liverpool; the Mariners Museum, Newport News; H. Matthews, Isle of Wight; the Peabody Museum, Salem; Tom Rayner, Ryde, Isle of Wight; Skyfotos Ltd., New Romney; Turners (Photography) Ltd., Newcastle on Tyne; the Walker Art Gallery, Liverpool; and the World Ship Photo Library.

A special thank you goes to Mr. C.J.M. Carter, the former Editor of the magazine *Sea Breezes* for all his help and encouragement throughout the years, and particularly with this project.

BIBLIOGRAPHY

Berry, A.C. *Unpublished letters*, Southend-on-Sea, 1976-1977.

Bibby, Brian *Unpublished letters*, Southampton, 1975-1977.

Binney, Hugh *Unpublished letters*, Cemaes Bay, 1974-1976 and Personal interviews, Cardiff, 1975.

Buenos Aires Herald, September 1876.

Cubbin, Capt. Graeme *Harrisons of Liverpool*, World Ship Society, Gravesend, and Ships in Focus Publications, Preston, 2003.

Devisate, Carlos Alberto (Editor) *O Porto de Santos Sua Historia*, Editora Documentacao Brasileira Ltda., Sao Paulo, 1986.

Dickinson, Capt. S. *Unpublished letters*, Hightown, Merseyside, 1976.

Dunn, Laurence *Merchant Ships of the World in Colour 1910-1929*, Blandford Press, 1973.

Edgar, Capt. T. *Unpublished letters*, Liverpool, 1976.

Evans, F. *Unpublished letters*, Rochdale, 1976-77.

Gangway, Journal of Blue Star Line, Booth Line and Lamport & Holt Line, 1974-1994.

Haikney, Capt. B.S. *Unpublished letters*, Wallasey, 1976.

Haws, Duncan *Merchant Fleets 14 Blue Star Line*, T.C.L. Publications, Hereford, 1988.

Haws, Duncan *Merchant Fleets 34 Lamport & Holt and Booth*, T.C.L. Publications, Uckfield, 1998.

Heaton, P.M. *Lamport & Holt Fleet*, serialised in Sea Breezes, June-December, 1977.

Heaton, P.M. *Lamport & Holt*, Author, Pontypool, 1986.

Heaton, P.M. *Booth Line*, Author, Pontypool, 1987.

H.M.S.O. *British Vessels Lost at Sea 1914-1918*, Reprinted by Patrick Stephens, Cambridge, 1977.

H.M.S.O. *British Vessels Lost at Sea 1939-1945*, Reprinted by Patrick Stephens, Cambridge, 1976.

Jones, Capt. J.I. DSO, DSC & Bar, *Personal interview*, Cardiff, 1975.

Jones, Clement *Pioneer Shipowners*, Charles Birchall, Liverpool, 1930

Lecky, Capt. S.T.S. *Wrinkles in Practical Navigation*, George Phillip, 1910.

Lloyd's Register of Shipping, Lloyd's Register.

Marine News, Journal of the World Ship Society, various issues, Kendal.

Martin, Capt. F. *Unpublished letters*, Meopham, 1975.

Metcalfe, Capt. B.M. *Unpublished letters*, Ambleside, 1975-1977.

Mitchell, W.H. and Sawyer, L.A. *Empire Ships of World War II*, Journal of Commerce, Liverpool, 1965.

Mitchell, W.H. and Sawyer, L.A. *The Oceans, The Forts & The Parks*, Journal of Commerce, Liverpool, 1967.

Mitchell, W.H. and Sawyer, L.A. *British Standard Ships of World War I*, Journal of Commerce, Liverpool, 1968.

Page, F.J. *Unpublished letters*, Wallasey, 1975-1976.

Roberts, Capt. D.C. *Unpublished letters*, Liverpool, 1976.

Roberts, Capt. G.E. *Unpublished letters*, Aberystwyth, 1976.

Roberts, M. *Unpublished letters*, Liverpool, 1974-1979.

Rohwer, Jurgen *Axis Submarine Successes 1939-1945*, Patrick Stephens, 1983.

Ross, L. *Unpublished letter*, Liverpool, 1976.

Sawyer, L.A. and Mitchell, W.H. *The Liberty Ships*, David & Charles, Newton Abbot, 1970.

Sawyer, L.A. and Mitchell, W.H. *Victory Ships and Tankers*, David & Charles, Newton Abbot, 1974.

Sea Breezes, various issues.

Sparks, Capt. W.A. *Unpublished letters*, Wallasey, 1976-1977.

Waring, T. *Unpublished letters*, Warrington, 1975.

Watson, Milton H. *Disasters at Sea*, Patrick Stephens, Wellingborough, 1987.

Woodward, David *The Secret Raiders*, William Kimber, 1955

Wright, Esther Clark, *Saint John Ships and Their Builders*, Author, Wolfville, Canada, 1976.

1. THE FOUNDERS - WILLIAM JAMES LAMPORT AND GEORGE HOLT

Established in 1845, the Lamport and Holt Line was the result of a partnership entered into by William James Lamport and George Holt.

Lamport, the senior partner, was born at Lancaster on the day of the Battle of Waterloo, June 18, 1815. His family origins can be traced back to France, thence via Devon to Lancashire, where his father was a Unitarian Minister. Subsequently in the 1830s he entered the offices at Liverpool of Messrs Gibbs, Bright and Company, who were friends of his family. It was with this company that he acquired a practical knowledge of commerce and ship management which was to later earn him a place among Liverpool's leading shipowners. His brother Charles became established as a shipbuilder at Workington, and a number of the partners' early sailing ships were built at this yard.

Much more is known of the other partner, George Holt. His family originated from Rochdale, a Lancashire textile town, from where his father George, senior (1790-1861), came in October 1807 to be apprenticed to a leading cotton broker Samuel Hope at premises in Water Street, Liverpool. In 1812 George senior was admitted as a partner in this business. In 1820 he married Emma Durning from whose family he rented a cottage in Rake Lane, Edge Hill. Three years later, by mutual agreement, George Holt senior and Samuel Hope separated their business interests. The latter entered banking whilst George remained in cotton, now trading as George Holt and Company.

George and Emma Holt had five sons; William who joined his father in the cotton business; George junior (born on September 19, 1824) who was to be co-founder of the Lamport & Holt Line; Alfred who served an apprenticeship to a railway engineer and later spent a

William James Lamport 1815-1874

period with Lamport & Holt before founding his own shipping company, later to be known as the Blue Funnel Line; Robert Durning who became the first Lord Mayor of Liverpool in 1883; and Philip Henry who initially had a small interest in Lamport and Holt, but eventually left to become a partner with Alfred. George junior was apprenticed in his youth to Thos. and Jno. Brocklebank, and it was whilst so serving that he met Lamport.

Having decided to enter shipowning, but also trading as brokers, charterers and merchants, Lamport who was now thirty years of age and the twenty-one year old Holt opened offices at Fenwick Buildings, Fenwick Street, Liverpool, but as the business grew they moved to larger premises in Drury Buildings, Water Street.

George Holt 1824-1896

2.   THE ENTRY INTO SHIPOWNING

The first Lamport & Holt ship, the barque *Christabel* of 335 tons was launched at Alexander's Workington shipyard on September 17, 1845 and was financed by George Holt's father who initially held over half the shares in her, but on November 14 of the same year he transferred his 34 shares to the two partners and it was thus that they became shipowners. George Holt senior was an extremely wealthy and influential gentleman, and gave his wholehearted support to the venture, as indeed he did with all that his sons were involved in. Although remaining in their ownership for just under a year before sale back to her builders, she was employed in the Alexandria cotton trade, bringing cargo back to Liverpool for the Lancashire cotton mills. Egyptian cotton being the best in the world was much in demand.

The partners' second ship was the barque *Junior* of 677 tons, built to their order at Quebec, and launched in the same year as the *Christabel*. Taken over on November 27, 1845 she sailed from Liverpool on December 23 under the command of Captain John Eills, who owned sixteen shares in her. This ship master was to hold shares in many of the partners' early ships, and was later to help Alfred Holt with the formation of his early fleet. This ship traded to Bombay, making annual voyages, but was lost in 1855, their first loss.

The smaller ships were normally employed in the Alexandria cotton trade, with the bigger vessels trading much further afield, Bombay, New Zealand, Australia, New Orleans and subsequently the East Coast of South America. Many relatives, friends and associates of the partners were to hold shares in these early ships. Each ship was divided into 64 shares, and the profits for each voyage, after the subtraction of expenses and management fees by Lamport & Holt, were divided between shareholders. As an example the share position of Lamport & Holt's third ship is given in detail. She was the full rigged ship *William Ward*, of 755 tons, built at St. John, New Brunswick, in 1842, and bought by the partners on March 10, 1846. The shareholders were as follows:

Date	Shareholders/Transactions	No. of Shares
10.3.1846	William James Lamport and George Holt the younger, trading as Lamport and Holt.	56
	Robert Bibby and Jas. Fisher	8
25.11.1846	Lamport and Holt transferred shares as follows:	
	to Thos. Fisher Moore	8
	to William Thornley	8
	to John Eills	4
19.6.1852	Thos. Fisher Moore transferred shares to Lamport and Holt	8
15.1.1853	Lamport and Holt transferred shares to Frederick McConnell	8
8.6.1853	The vessel was sold to William Morgan of Liverpool.	

Prior to 1850 eleven sailing ships had been acquired, only one of which had been disposed of. An interesting ship dating from 1845 when built at Sunderland for George Holt senior, was the full rigged ship *Emma* which passed to Lamport & Holt in 1847. A painting of this vessel housed in the Sudley Art Gallery and Museum at Liverpool clearly shows the Lamport & Holt houseflag which remained unchanged throughout the history of the firm. The vessel was named after George Holt senior's wife.

The full rigged ship *Emma* entered the Lamport & Holt fleet in 1847.   *(Walker Art Gallery - Artist unknown)*

FLEET LIST Part 1

Name & Period in Fleet	Gross tons	History
Christabel (1) 1845-1846	335	Barque. 1845 built by James Alexander, Workington, for George Holt, Cotton Broker, Liverpool; 1845 to Lamport & Holt; 1846 to James Alexander, Workington; 1847 to Harding, London; 1852 to Stranack, London; 1857 condemned and broken up.
Junior 1845-1855	677	Barque. 1845 built at Quebec for Lamport & Holt; 1855 wrecked.
William Ward 1846-1853	755	Ship. 1842 built by James Smith, St. John, for own account; 1846 to Lamport & Holt; 1853 to Wm. Morgan, Liverpool; 5.1855 lost at sea.
Julius Caesar 1846-1853	738	Ship. 1838 built at New Brunswick, for Black Ball Line; 1846 to Lamport & Holt; 1853 condemned and broken up.
Emma 1847-1852	376	Ship. 1845 built at Sunderland, for George Holt, Cotton Broker, Liverpool; 1847 to Lamport & Holt; 1852 to Schillizzi, Liverpool; 1860 to J. Smurthwaite, Sunderland; 1963 to G. Seymour, London; 1866 to J. Snowdon, South Shields; 1874 broken up.

Name & Period in Fleet	Gross tons	History
Grasmere 1847-1865	454	Ship. 1847 built at Chepstow for Lamport & Holt; 1865 lost at sea.
Moslem 1848-1853	170	Brig. 1835 built at Yarmouth for J. Vale, London; 1848 to Lamport & Holt; 1853 to T. Blessett, Liverpool; 1858 broken up at Tranmere.
Thornhill 1848-1856	698	Ship. 1848 built at Quebec for Lamport & Holt; 1856 omitted, no other details.
Napan Belle 1849-1856	332	Barque. 1849 built at Nova Scotia and following her maiden Atlantic crossing to Liverpool with a timber cargo, sold to Lamport & Holt; 1856 condemned and broken up.
Wilhelmina 1849-1852	168	Brig. 1843 built by Huddleston, Ritson and Company, for Seymour, Maryport; 1846 to James Moss and Company, Liverpool!; 1849 to Lamport & Holt; 1852 to Byers and Company, Workington; 1860 abandoned.
Balkan 1849-1863	192	Brigantine. 1849 built at Liverpool, for Lamport & Holt; 1863 to Gambles, Liverpool; 1865 wrecked in the West Indies.

3. JAMES MOSS AND COMPANY – JOINT MEDITERRANEAN SERVICE

The next few years were to see great developments on the Mersey. Lamport & Holt had close connections with James Moss and Company, and were in fact trading in a joint service to the Mediterranean. James Moss and Company acquired their first three steamships for this service, and much of the specification for the vessels was undertaken by the Engineering Department of Lamport & Holt, who took shares in all three of them. The actual shareholdings are reproduced hereunder. The steamer *Nile*, built of iron by Alexandra Denny and Brother of Dumbarton was of 347 gross tons.

Date	Shareholders/Transactions	No. of Shares
13.11.1850	Registered at Liverpool, owner being William Miles Moss, trading as James Moss & Company	64
16.11.1850	William Miles Moss transferred shares to William James Lamport and George Holt the younger trading as Lamport and Holt	8
1.4.1851	William Miles Moss transferred shares to Lamport and Holt	16
2.7.1851	Lamport and Holt transferred shares to George Holt, Cotton Broker	2
	to Charles Booth, senior	2
	to Jas Thornely	1
	to Wm. Schaw Lindsay	2
17.5.1851	Lamport and Holt transferred shares to Thomas Fisher Moore	3
4.4.1853	Vessel sold and re-registered at Dublin.	

It is interesting to note the appearance of Lamport's cousin Charles Booth, the Corn Merchant, as two of his sons, Alfred (1850-1857) and Charles (1855-1862) both served their time in the offices of Lamport & Holt, prior to entering business on their own account. The younger Holt brother Phillip was to marry their sister.

The *Orontes* built by the same builders as the *Nile*, but the following year, for James Moss and Company, had the following shareholders initially.

Shareholders	No. of Shares
Frederick Chapple	22
William Miles Moss	21
William James Lamport and George Holt the younger trading as Lamport and Holt	7
George Holt, the elder, cotton broker	2
Charles Booth, Senior	1
Wm. Rathbone and Samuel Martin, jointly	2
Wm. Rathbone Wm. Rathbone, the younger, Samuel Greg Rathbone, and Thomas Kenyon Twist, jointly trading as Rathbone Brothers	4
John Eills	2
Wm. Schaw Lindsay, London	2
Frederick McConnell	1

Alfred Holt, who was in charge of Lamport & Holt's Engineering Department, had a great deal to do with the design of the *Orontes*, and sailed in her late in 1851 on her maiden voyage to Egypt. On his return he spent much time on the design of the next Moss steamer, *Scamander* of 753 gross tons, built in 1854 by Stothert and Company, Clifton, Gloucestershire, another iron steamer. The initial shareholders in the *Scamander* were as follows:

Shareholders	No. of Shares
Wm. Miles Moss and Frederick Chapple, jointly	52
William James Lamport and George Holt the younger trading as Lamport and Holt	4
Wm. Rathbone, Wm. Rathbone, the younger, Samuel Greg Rathbone, and Thomas Kenyon Twist, trading as Rathbone Brothers	4
Wm. Schaw Lindsay	4

Clearly most of the above people held shares in each other's ships, and also had an interest in Lamport & Holt's early venture into shipowning.

In 1857 Lamport & Holt acquired the 189 ton steamer *Zulu* from Scott and Company, Greenock, initially for service off South Africa, but in the event served in the West Indies, for a short period as a feeder ship to Alfred Holt's small fleet involved in this highly competitive trade. This ship was sold in 1858, although Lamport & Holt were operating seventeen sailing ships worldwide, with a still active participation in the Alexandria trade.

Alfred Holt had left to establish his own business, operating from offices at India Buildings, Liverpool. In 1857 Alfred Booth left Lamport & Holt and spent three years at Rathbone Brother's New York office, before establishing himself in the tanning business initially at New York and later co-founded the Booth Line with his brother Charles.

During the Crimean War the British Government chartered considerable tonnage, using steamers, and those of James Moss as transports for troops and cavalry, and sailing ships for stores. It was whilst so employed that the *Simoda* a 697 ton full rigged ship was wrecked in the Dardanelles in February, 1856. She was soon replaced in the fleet by the 1,023 ton *Agenoria* bought new, and which later held the distinction of being the first ship to call at a Brazilian port to top off with cargo, albeit unscheduled.

FLEET LIST Part 2

Name & Period in Fleet	Gross tons	History
Cathaya 1850-1857	407	Ship. 1850 built by Charles Lamport, Workington, for Lamport & Holt; 1852 lengthened, tonnage increased to 503; 1857 lost at sea.
Ceres 1850-1856	117	Schooner. 1850 built at Prince Edward Island, for Lamport & Holt; 1856 to T. Colgan, Hull; 1862 to Blaney and Company, Glasgow; 1870 damaged by grounding and broken up.
Jane Morice 1850-1870	323	Barque. 1850 built at New Brunswick, for Lamport & Holt; 1870 omitted, no details.
Margaret Gibson 1850-1866	124	Brig. 1844 built at Hull, for W. Gibson, Hull; 1850 to Lamport & Holt; lengthened, tonnage increased to 148; 1866 omitted, no details.

Name & Period in Fleet	Gross tons	History
Rydal 1852	262	Barque. 1852 built by Isaac J. & W.G. Olive, New Brunswick and on arrival at Liverpool sold on their behalf by W.J. Lamport to Rathbone Bros., Liverpool; 1864 destroyed by fire.
Princeza 1853-1862	149	Brig. 1849 built at Aberdeen, for Miller and Company, Liverpool; 1853 to Lamport & Holt; 1862 to unknown owners; 1870 wrecked.
Queen 1854-1859	104	Schooner. 1848 built at Teignmouth, for A. Owen, Teignmouth; 1854 to Lamport & Holt; 1859 to Pritchard, Bangor; 1863 lost.
Simoda 1855-1856	697	Ship. 1854 built by Wm. Potts, St. John, for J. Kirk Jnr & G.W. Worrall, St. John, and on arrival at Liverpool after her maiden crossing to Lamport & Holt; 1856 wrecked off Dardanelles.
Breeze 1855-1868	165	Snow. 1848 built at Annan, for J. Nicholson, Annan; 1855 to Lamport & Holt; 1868 went missing.
Agenoria 1856-1868	1,023	Ship. 1856 built by James Thomas Smith, New Brunswick, for own account; on arrival at Liverpool to Lamport & Holt; 1868 to Griffiths and Company, Liverpool; 1868 to Young and Company, North Shields; 1885 broken up at North Shields.

4. THE LIVERPOOL, BRAZIL AND RIVER PLATE STEAM NAVIGATION CO. LTD.

In 1861 the partners bowed to the inevitable, and ordered two brig-rigged iron steamers. The *Memnon* (1,290 gross tons) was delivered in 1861 by Scott and Company, Greenock, and the *Copernicus* (1,372 gross tons) was completed the following year by A. Leslie and Company, Hebburn-on-Tyne. This shipyard was to deliver a considerable number of vessels to the partners over the next three decades. These ships were employed in the joint service with James Moss and Company to the Mediterranean where their increased capacity was found to be most useful. These ships also introduced passenger accommodation to the Lamport & Holt fleet. However the fleet was still acquiring sailing ships for the Mediterranean and worldwide trades, and continued to do so for some years to come. It was these early steamers which introduced the practice of naming ships after prominent persons connected with the arts and sciences.

For some considerable time both Alfred Holt, who was now fairly established on his own account, and Phillip Henry Holt, who held a small interest in Lamport & Holt, had been urging Lamport, the senior partner, to start a really good steamship line in one of the Atlantic trades. Lamport took a good deal of persuasion, for although his attitude to steamers had changed, he still did not believe in lines of steamers. But eventually he yielded and ordered a new vessel from Andrew Leslie and Company specifically for the Brazil and River Plate trade. She was an iron, brig-rigged steamer of 1,500 gross tons, completed in 1863 and named *Kepler*. Having taken a great interest in her construction, Alfred Holt sailed in her on her maiden voyage to Brazil and the River Plate via Lisbon, leaving Liverpool on July 18.

Clement Jones in his book *Pioneer Shipowners* refers to this new venture:

> From a small beginning that huge Brazil and River Plate undertaking was started against the wish (or with the complete indifference) of Lamport and Holt, and owing to the persistence of Alfred and Philip Henry Holt. A study of the history of shipping shows us that some are born to a trade, others acquire trades, while some like Mr. Lamport have trades thrust upon them.

January, 1864 saw the termination of Philip Henry Holt's connection with the partners, and he joined his brother Alfred in the management of his company from India Buildings, Liverpool. Thereafter they made the plans and laid the foundations for their important service to the Far East. However, it is interesting to note that when there was a temporary slump in their trade, as occurred from time to time, that one or more of their ships was placed on the Lamport & Holt berth for a voyage or voyages to the East Coast of South America.

The enterprise had developed so well, and the size of the fleet was growing so rapidly that the partners decided to form a limited company under the title of 'The Liverpool, Brazil and River Plate Steam Navigation Company Limited', of which the partnership became managers. This transaction took effect from December 18, 1865. Previously the ships had been operated on the 64 shares system, whereby the voyage profits less management fees and expenses of each vessel were divided amongst shareholders in specific vessels. Under the new system the shareholders were allocated shares in the new company, and received dividends from the profits of the company as a whole. This was a far less risky proposition, as under the old system shareholders could be liable for unlimited losses, whereas with a limited company they were only liable for their actual shareholding. Whilst this was the arrangement for the steamer fleet, the 64 share system was maintained for their sailing vessels with which they were to remain involved for over a decade to come.

The growth of the fleet was rapid. In 1868 they were awarded the contract by Brazil for mail to and from that country which within five years resulted in weekly sailings. This was followed by a contract with the British Postmaster General for mail to and from Argentina requiring monthly sailings. In truth, these were the minimum requirements, and sailings were now being made from London, Antwerp and Glasgow as well as Liverpool.

In 1869 the steamer *Halley* became the first iron steamer to transport a coffee shipment from Rio de Janeiro to New York, thus breaking with the old idea that it would spoil the flavour to carry coffee in anything other than a wooden sailing ship. This was a turning point in the company's affairs, in that they now started trading direct from the River Plate and Brazil to United States East Coast ports, and on occasions returned back to South America, or to the United Kingdom with the raw materials for the cotton industry.

Alas in 1874 William James Lamport died aged 59 years at his home at New Brighton. His place in the partnership was taken by Walter Holland who had served the company since the end of his apprenticeship alongside Lamport at Gibbs, Bright and Company. Another partner was appointed, that being their longest serving employee, Charles Jones. At Lamport's death the fleet numbered 31 vessels of 48,236 gross tons.

Some idea of the importance of Lamport & Holt can be seen in the following advertisement which appeared in the first issue of the English language newspaper, the Buenos Aires Herald in September, 1876. As can be seen passengers, both saloon and steerage, were carried in all vessels, and a surgeon on all of the ships. Lamport & Holt was by far the largest carrier from South America to and from the United Kingdom, Belgium and the United States.

STEAM TO NEW YORK

Lamport and Holt's Line of Steamers
Under contract with the Brazilian Government
The splendid steamship
Tycho Brahe
1,848 tons
Miller, Commander
Will leave this Port on the 18th
September for

NEW YORK

via Rio de Janeiro, Bahia and Pernambuco and Para
(leaving Rio de Janeiro on 1st October)

Rates of Passage Money

	1st class	3rd class
New York	$.197.20	$.85.40
Para	130	49
Pernambuco	90	40
Bahia	70	35
Rio de Janeiro	50	25

All the steamers of this Line are repleted with every comfort, and carry a Surgeon and a Stewardess.

Liverpool, Brazil and River Plate Steamers
Lamport and Holt's Line
Departures
S.S. *Kepler,* for Havre and Liverpool
Will leave on 15th September.

S.S. *Tycho Brahe*, for New York
Will leave on the 18th September
and Rio de Janeiro 1st October.

————

S.S. *Hipparchus*, for Antwerp and Liverpool
Will leave this port on 25th September
(carrying the Belgian Mails.)

————

S.S. *Delambre*, for Antwerp and Liverpool
Will leave this port on 30th September
Receiving Cargo in the River Parana.

————

S.S. *Hevelius*, for Antwerp and Liverpool
Will leave on Monday, 9th October
(carrying the Belgian Mails.)

————

Rates of Passage Money		
	1st	3rd
Southampton, Liverpool, Havre and Antwerp	£35	£15
Lisbon	30	12
Bahia	12	7
Rio de Janeiro	10	5
New York	40	17.10

In the Mail Steamers Table Wine is supplied gratis to all passengers.
First Class Return Tickets are issued (with a reduction of 25%),
available for 12 months.
All the steamers of this Line carry Surgeons and Stewardesses, and
are replete with every comfort.

————

FLEET LIST Part 3

Name & Period in Fleet	Gross tons	History
Levant 1856	1,210	Ship. 1856 built by F.J. & T. Ruddock, St. John, and sold on their behalf by W.J. Lamport to Rathbone Bros., Liverpool; 1.10.1871 foundered.
Kahlamba 1856-1869	319	Iron Barque. 1856 built by J. Reid and Company, Port Glasgow, for Lamport & Holt; 1869 to C. de Casas, Rivadeo, renamed *Carlos*; 1884 to John Craig, Greenock, renamed *Kahlamba*; 1885 to Peter Scott, Greenock; 1887 to J. O'Connor, Buenos Aires; 1890 omitted – possibly hulked.
Memphis 1856-1862	416	Barque. 1856 built by Ruddock Bros., St. John, for Lamport & Holt; 1862 to Phillips and Company, Liverpool; 1871 to Whitby owners; 4.1884 wrecked at Bornholm.
Zulu 1857-1858	189	Steamship. 1857 built by Scott and Company, Greenock, for Lamport & Holt; 1858 to Mauritius owners; 28.5.1861 lost off Jamaica.
Blencathra 1857-1874	466	Barque. 1857 built by Charles Lamport, Workington, for Lamport & Holt; 1871 to W.J. Lamport; 1874 broken up.
Coniston 1857-1865	204	Barque. 1857 built by Charles Lamport, Workington, for Lamport & Holt; 1865 wrecked.
Elizabeth Morrow 1857-1860	394	Barque. 1857 built by Cait and Son, New Brunswick, and following first Atlantic crossing to Liverpool, bought by Lamport & Holt; 1860 to Walker and Company, Glasgow; 1864 to Cornish and Company Liverpool; 1870 omitted.
Glaramara 1857-1863	475	Barque. 1857 built by Charles Lamport, Workington, for Lamport & Holt; 1863 to Shute and Company, Liverpool; 1865 to Hudson Bay Company, London; 1867 to Brymner and Company, Greenock; 1870 lost by fire.
Old Harry 1857-1870	156	Ketch. 1843 built at Maidstone for C. Pubus, Rochester; 1857 to Lamport & Holt; 1870 omitted.
Rothay 1858-1864	198	Schooner. 1858 built by Charles Lamport, Workington, for Lamport & Holt; 1864 to J. Hainsworth, Liverpool; 1874 broken up.
Thebes 1858-1862	432	Barque. 1850 built at Sunderland, for Rathbone and Company, Liverpool; 1858 to Lamport & Holt; 1862 to E.S. Roberts, London; 1863 to Weinhoft and Company, London; 1865 abandoned at sea.
Labrador 1858	1,242	Ship. 1858 built by F.J. & T. Ruddock, St. John, and sold on their behalf by Lamport & Holt to Rathbone Bros., Liverpool; later sold to Williams & Roberts Cambrian Line; 1877 to Greenock owners; 1886 went missing.
Sir John Mandeville 1859-1877	1,379	Ship. 1859 built by James Thomas Smith, New Brunswick, for Lamport & Holt; 1877 to Norwegian owners, renamed *Magnum*; 1895 wrecked.

Name & Period in Fleet	Gross tons	History
Canova (1) 1859	1,283	Ship. 1859 built by F.J. & T. Ruddock, St. John, and sold on their behalf by Lamport & Holt to Rathbone Bros., Liverpool; 1864 to J. Fleming, Glasgow; 1872 to T.R. Miller, Newcastle; 1885 to T. Emerson, Newcastle; 1891 broken up.
Eddystone 1860-1861	526	Barque. 1860 built by Thomas Hilyard, New Brunswick, and sold on their behalf in 1861 to Young and Son, South Shields, renamed *St. Mirren*; 1862 to J. Avery, North Shields; 1873 omitted.
Attila 1860-1864	1,146	Ship. 1860 built by Thomas Hilyard, New Brunswick, for Lamport & Holt; 1864 to William Rathbone, Liverpool; 1871 to Middle Dock Company, Newcastle as a store ship; 1885 to J.L. Tonnessen, Lillesand, renamed *Atila*; 1885 omitted.
Memnon 1861-1883	1,290	Steamship. 1861 built by Scott and Company, Greenock, for Lamport & Holt; 1865 to Liverpool, Brazil & River Plate Steam Navigation Co. Ltd. (Lamport & Holt); 1872 new engine and boiler fitted; 1883 to Ocean Steamship Co. Ltd. (Alfred Holt and Company); 1893 to East India Ocean Steamship Co. Ltd. (Alfred Holt and Company), Dutch flag; 1899 hulked at Singapore.
Bonnie Dundee 1861-1872	1,027	Ship. 1861 built by McLachlan & Stackhouse, New Brunswick, for Lamport & Holt; 1872 to T. Spaight, Limerick; 1879 to H. Ewing, Liverpool; 1882 to H.M. Rummelhoff, Christiania, renamed *Signe*; 1890 broken up.
Thalaba 1861	940	Ship. 1861 built by F.J. & T. Ruddock, St. John, and sold on their behalf to Scarborough owners; no other details.
Copernicus (1) 1862-1864	1,372	Steamship. 1862 built by Andrew Leslie and Company, Hebburn, for Lamport & Holt; 1864 to Messageries Imperiales, Marseilles, renamed *Copernic*; 1871 owners restyled at Messageries Maritimes; 1.1890 broken up at Marseilles.
Chalgrove 1862-1869	509	Barque. 1862 built by Charles Lamport, Workington, for Lamport & Holt; 1869 to R. Habgood, London; 1878 to Mrs E.Habgood (widow); 1886 to W. Garrett, London; 1889 to Bevan, Evans and Company, London; 1893 to H.J. Larsen, Lillesand; 1896 broken up.
Nazarine 1862-1865	921	Ship. 1854 built at Quebec for Fisher and Sons, Liverpool; 1862 to Lamport & Holt; 1865 to Curwin and Company, Liverpool; 1869 to W. Geves; 1872 lost at sea.
Hampden 1862-1871	1,499	Ship. 1862 built by F.J. & T. Ruddock, St. John, for Lamport & Holt; 1871 to owners at North Shields; 1874 to Glasgow owners; 9.1877 abandoned on fire on a voyage from Leith to Bombay.
Kepler 1863-1903	1,500	Steamship. 1863 built by Andrew Leslie and Company, Hebburn, for Lamport & Holt; 1865 to Liverpool, Brazil & River Plate Steam Navigation Co. Ltd. (Lamport & Holt); 1871 lengthened and new engines and boilers fitted, tonnage increased to 2,258; 1878 to Societe de Navigation Royale Belge Sud-Americaine (Lamport & Holt) Antwerp; 1902 to Liverpool, Brazil & River Plate Steam Navigation Co. Ltd. (Lamport & Holt); 1903 broken up.

Name & Period in Fleet	Gross tons	History
Christabel (2) 1863-1864	170	Brigantine. 1863 built by Owen, Teignmouth, for Lamport & Holt; 1864 to H.F. Watt, Liverpool; 1869 to Tonge and Company, Liverpool; 1870 to R. Gladstone, Liverpool; 1876 to Baine and Johnston, Greenock; 1885 to W.B. Grieve, Greenock; 1887 to M. Lawrey, Plymouth; 1897 to J. Randell, Plymouth; 8.1903 hulked at Plymouth.
Samarang 1863	1,175	Ship. 1857 built by F.J. & T. Ruddock, St. John, for their own account; 1859 to Rathbone Bros., Liverpool; 1863 to Lamport & Holt; 1863 to Newcastle owners; 10.1884 wrecked on Saltburn Beach.
Arethuse 1864	1,184	Steamship. 1864 built by Samuda Bros., London; laid down for Lamport & Holt, but completed for Messageries Imperiales, Marseilles.
Newton (1) 1864-1881	1,329	Steamship. 1864 built by McNab and Company, Greenock, for Lamport & Holt; 1865 to Liverpool, Brazil & River Plate Steam Navigation Co. Ltd. (Lamport & Holt); 9.4.1881 wrecked off Madeira, while on passage Rio de Janeiro to London.
Galileo (1) 1864-1869	1,585	Steamship. 1864 built by Andrew Leslie and Company, Hebburn, for Lamport & Holt; 1865 to Liverpool, Brazil & River Plate Steam Navigation Co. Ltd. (Lamport & Holt); 1869 to T.H. Jackson, Liverpool, renamed *Juan*; 1874 to J. Jack and Company, Liverpool, who re-engined her, completing same the following year; 1878 to J.B. Palmer and Company, London; 1882 to W. Banks, London; 1884 T.A. Hinton, London; 1888 to Westcott and Lawrence; 1898 to H. Diederichsen, Kiel; 26.8.1898 sailed from Hong Kong for Kiaochow, and went missing.

The *Galileo* (1) was built by Andrew Leslie and Company, Hebburn-on-Tyne, for Lamport & Holt in 1864.

Name & Period in Fleet	Gross tons	History
Brunette 1864	1,508	Ship. 1864 built by Thomas Hilyard, New Brunswick, for Lamport & Holt, and following her initial Atlantic crossing to Liverpool, resold to Rathbone Bros., Liverpool, renamed *Irwell*; 1872 to G.C. Trufant, London; 1880 abandoned water logged in the North Atlantic.
Saladin 1865-1872	510	Steamship. 1856 built by Cato, Miller and Company, Liverpool, for Alfred Holt & Company, Liverpool; 1864 to West India & Pacific Steamship Company; 1865 to Liverpool, Brazil & River Plate Steam Navigation Co. Ltd. (Lamport & Holt); 1872 to J. Martin, Liverpool; 1882 broken up.
Talisman 1865-1873	738	Steamship. 1860 built by Scott and Company, Greenock, for Alfred Holt & Company, Liverpool; 1864 to West India & Pacific Steamship Company; 1865 to Liverpool, Brazil & River Plate Steam Navigation Co. Ltd. (Lamport & Holt); 21.1.1873 foundered North West of Burlings, Portugal.
Ptolemy 1865-1896	1,401	Steamship. 1865 built by Andrew Leslie and Company, Hebburn, for Liverpool, Brazil & River Plate Steam Navigation Co. Ltd. (Lamport & Holt); 1880 re-engined; 1896 broken up.

The *Ptolemy* was built in 1865 for the Liverpool, Brazil and River Plate Steam Navigation Co. Ltd. This photograph is the earliest I have seen of a Lamport & Holt ship, hence the quality.

Name & Period in Fleet	Gross tons	History
Halley 1865-1895	1,637	Steamship. 1865 built by Andrew Leslie and Company, Hebburn, for Liverpool, Brazil & River Plate Steam Navigation Co. Ltd. (Lamport & Holt); 1895 broken up by T.W. Ward, Preston.
Herschel (1) 1865-1872	1,240	Steamship. 1853 built by Laird Bros., Birkenhead, for the African Steamship Co. Ltd., Liverpool, but sold while fitting out to Canadian Steamship Co. Ltd., Liverpool, as *Charity*; 1856 to Lineas de Vapores Correos Espanoles Transatlanticos, Cadiz, renamed *La Cubano*; 1865 to Liverpool, Brazil & River Plate Steam Navigation Co. Ltd. (Lamport & Holt), renamed *Herschel*; 1872 to R.M. Sloman and Company, Hamburg, converted to a sailing ship and renamed *Palmerston*; 1890 to Bruckner and Albers, Hamburg; 1894 to A. Princeti, Genoa, renamed *Frederico*; 1899 condemned, broken up at Genoa.
Sumroo 1865-1867	612	Barque. 1865 built by Thomas Hilyard, New Brunswick, for Lamport & Holt; 1867 to unknown German owners; 1871 omitted.
Timour 1865	1,331	Ship. 1865 built by Thomas Hilyard, New Brunswick, for Lamport & Holt; 1865 to Rathbone Bros., Liverpool; 1872 to Fernie and Company, Liverpool; 1881 to Alexander Cassels, Liverpool; 1877 converted to a barque; 1882 to W.H. Ross and Company, Liverpool; 1882 to Limerick owners; 11.1882 wrecked on Prince Edward Island.
Chiltern 1865	1,141	Ship. 1865 built by F.J. & T. Ruddock, St. John, as *Chiltern* for Lamport & Holt; following delivery voyage sold to Stoddart's of Liverpool, renamed *Vanda*; 1870 lost by fire in coal cargo.
Ironsides 1866-1868	691	Steamship. 1865 built by Candlish and Company, Middlesbrough, for Girvin and Company, Liverpool; 1866 to Lamport & Holt; 1868 to D. Jones, Briton Ferry; 1869 to Stowe and Company, Cardiff; 1874 omitted.

The collier *Ironsides* – early master, Captain S.T.C. Lecky

The collier *Ironsides* is of interest, as a short account of her early master appears in the foreword of a navigation book entitled *Wrinkles in Practical Navigation* by Captain S.T.C. Lecky, Master Mariner, Commander RNR., FRAS., FRGS,. Extra Master; Younger Brother, Trinity House; from which the following passage is quoted:

During 1865 this company was wound up, and at the end of August his connection with the *Krishna* perforce came to an end. 'But' wrote the indomitable Lecky, 'my luck still held good, for I immediately got command of a screw collier, trading between Liverpool, Cardiff and elsewhere'.

This vessel was the *Ironsides* of 514 tons, belonging to Mr. Robert Girvan, of Liverpool. What luck indeed. There are few sailors who would consider themselves fortunate in having given up the Inman Line (a reference to the company with which he served before his service in the *Krishna*) to find themselves on board a collier.

He admitted however in later years that, luck or no luck, although it had not been pleasant work, it had given him fresh opportunities and new experience in a strange trade. It was his first real command, and he was undoubtedly fortunate in getting even such a humble one within so short a time of obtaining his master's certificate (September 13, 1864; extra master's certificate October 27, 1864. He was also qualified in the Board of Trade examination in steam machinery). The experience added greatly to his general usefulness and to the store of knowledge of all classes of ships which he was accumulating.

On February 17, 1866, the screw collier master, now in his 28th year, was gazetted a sub-lieutenant in the Royal Naval Reserve, and for various periods in1867 and early 1868, while his ship was discharging, he was devoting his short holidays to putting in his drills on board HMS *Eagle* at Liverpool; and having satisfactorily qualified he was gazetted as a Lieutenant RNR to date January 14, 1868.

'Those were the days', he wrote, 'in which there was no retaining fees for RNR officers, nor was there any allowance for uniform and equipment, so I spent far more on the RNR than ever returned to me'.

It will be within the experience of many that, if treated loyally, a humble appointment very often becomes the stepping stone to something a good deal better, and it was a source of considerable gratification to Lecky to find suddenly that his inconspicuous collier had been purchased by Messrs. Lamport and Holt, the well known shipowners of Liverpool, who were trading as the Liverpool, Brazil and River Plate Steam Navigation Co. Ltd., and who retained him as master and kept on all his officers. He remained in the *Ironsides* for another eight months with his new owners and left her on August 17, 1867.

Thenceforward his career ran pleasantly enough in the well-equipped, comfortable steamers of this great company trading between Liverpool and the principal ports of Eastern South America. He commanded successively over a period of four years their steamships:– *Ironsides; Cassini*, 687 tons – three months; the chartered ship *Uruguay*, 856 tons – thirteen months; and the *Halley*, 995 tons – sixteen months; and became well known in connection with them.

He resigned his position in the *Halley* at Liverpool on October 21, 1870, following a dispute with George Holt, in which, from the text of this foreword, it would appear that Mr. Lamport disagreed with his partner. Whatever, Lamport sent Lecky £100 from his own pocket, but Lecky would not return to the company.

Name & Period in Fleet	Gross tons	History
Cassini 1866-1871	993	Steamship. 1866 built by Andrew Leslie and Company, Hebburn, for Liverpool, Brazil & River Plate Steam Navigation Co. Ltd. (Lamport & Holt); 1871 to R.T. Smyth and Company, Liverpool, later shown as Paul and Smyth; 1876 to Barrow Shipbuilding Company, Barrow; 1877 to Carruthers and Johnston, Liverpool; 1879 back to Barrow Shipbuilding Company, Barrow; 1881 to Navigazione Generale Italiana, Genoa; 1.1909 broken up at Palermo.
Copernicus (2) 1866-1883	1,629	Steamship. 1866 built by Andrew Leslie and Company, Hebburn, for Liverpool, Brazil & River Plate Steam Navigation Co. Ltd. (Lamport & Holt); 1877 to Societe de Navigation Royale Belge Sud-Americaine (Lamport & Holt), Antwerp; 2.1883 wrecked at Porto de Pedras, while on passage Liverpool to Bahia.
La Plata 1866-1874	1,394	Steamship. 1866 built by Palmers and Company, Jarrow for Malcolmson Bros., Waterford; 1866 to Liverpool, Brazil & River Plate Steam Navigation Co. Ltd. (Lamport & Holt); 1874 to Bailey and Leatham, Hull; 1875 re-engined; 3.7.1886 wrecked near Thisted, while on passage Tyne to Reval.
Donati 1866-1891	1,395	Steamship. 1866 built by Andrew Leslie and Company, Hebburn, for Liverpool, Brazil & River Plate Steam Navigation Co. Ltd. (Lamport & Holt); 1891 to A. Coote, and Company, Liverpool; 10.12.1892 went missing while on passage New York to Oporto.
Flamsteed (1) 1866-1873	1,376	Steamship. 1866 built by Andrew Leslie and Company, Hebburn, for Liverpool, Brazil & River Plate Steam Navigation Co. Ltd. (Lamport & Holt); 24.11.1873 lost in collision with HMS *Bellerphon*.

Name & Period in Fleet	Gross tons	History
Laplace (1) 1866-1894	1,410	Steamship. 1866 built by Andrew Leslie and Company, Hebburn, for Liverpool, Brazil & River Plate Steam Navigation Co. Ltd. (Lamport & Holt); 1874 new engine and boiler fitted; 8.1894 to Comp. Pernambuco de Nav., Pernambuco, renamed *Capibaribe*; 1917 broken up.
Humboldt 1866-1894	1,638	Steamship. 1866 built by Andrew Leslie and Company, Hebburn, for Liverpool, Brazil & River Plate Steam Navigation Co. Ltd. (Lamport & Holt); 1880 new engine and boiler fitted; 1894 to Comp. Pernambuco de Nav., Pernambuco, renamed *Camocim*; 1917 broken up.
March 1866-1867	1,255	Ship. 1866 built by Thomas Hilyard, New Brunswick, and sold on their behalf by Lamport & Holt to Charles Hill & Son, Bristol, in 1867 and renamed *Glenhaven*; 1872 to W. Rankin, Greenock; 1877 to V. Trayes, Cardiff; 1884 broken up.
Manchester 1866-1873	158	Brigantine. 1824 built at Whitehaven, for Brocklebank, Whitehaven; 1852 to Armstrong, Workington; 1866 to Lamport & Holt; 1873 broken up.
Southern Queen 1866-1880	789	Ship. 1866 built by F.J. & T. Ruddock, St. John, as *Blonde* for their own account; following delivery voyage to Liverpool, bought by Lamport & Holt, renamed *Southern Queen*; 1880 to Jenkins and Company, Liverpool, reduced to a barque; 1888 to O. Lohne, Mandel; 1895 broken up.
Tycho Brahe 1867-1892	1,808	Steamship. 1867 built by Andrew Leslie and Company, Hebburn, for Liverpool, Brazil & River Plate Steam Navigation Co. Ltd. (Lamport & Holt); 1878 to Societe de Navigation Royale Belge Sud-Americaine (Lamport & Holt), Antwerp; 1892 to Charles Wells and Company, London, renamed *Palais Royale*; 1893 to William Hurlbatt, London; 1894 to Idarei Massousieh, Constantinople, renamed *Taif*; 30.10.1908 lost in collision with steamer *Bagdad*, off Seraglio Point, Constantinople.

This painting of the steamer *Tycho Brahe* of 1867 was displayed for many years at the Dock office at No. 78, Irlam Road, Bootle. The vessel was sold in 1892 to Charles Wells of London – the man who broke the Bank at Monte Carlo. he appropriately renamed her *Palais Royale*.

Name & Period in Fleet	Gross tons	History
Hipparchus 1867-1915	1,863	Steamship. 1867 built by Andrew Leslie and Company, Hebburn, for Liverpool, Brazil & River Plate Steam Navigation Co. Ltd. (Lamport & Holt); 1878 to Societe de Navigation Royale Belge Sud-Americaine (Lamport & Holt), Antwerp; 1895 converted to a hulk at Valparaiso; 1.8.1915 sold, 2004 believed still afloat.
Christabel (3) 1867-1869	660	Barque. 1867 built by King, New Brunswick, and operated on their behalf by Lamport & Holt; 1869 sold on builder's behalf to Dubois and Burqueue, Nantes, renamed *Formose*; 1888 omitted.
Tidal Wave 1867-1868	1,280	Ship. 1867 built by King, New Brunswick, for Lamport & Holt; 1868 to Fletcher and Parr, Liverpool, renamed *Louisa Fletcher*; 1879 to C.S. Caird, Greenock; 1883 to A. Tischbein and Company, Lussinpiccolo, renamed *Florida*; 1890 to C.H. Evenson, Fredrikstad; 1892 abandoned in sinking condition in the Atlantic.
Florentine 1868-1870	979	Ship. 1868 built by Thomas Hilyard, New Brunswick, for W.J. Lamport, then transferred to Lamport & Holt; 1870 to Owen Edwards, Pwllheli; 1873 to H. Pugh and Company, Pwllheli; 2.9.1875 sighted off Angier, while on a voyage from Java to United Kingdom with a sugar cargo, and went missing.
West Riding 1868-1870	1,089	Ship. 1864 built by John McDonald, St. Johns, as *Edith* for their own account; 1864 sold on their behalf by Lamport & Holt to Thomas Seddon, renamed *West Riding*; 1868 to Lamport & Holt; 11.1870 condemned at Akyab with hull rot; replanked locally and sold for further trading; 1871 renamed *Stamboul*, no other details.
Mornington 1868	1,360	Ship. 1868 built by F.J. & T. Ruddock, St. John, and sold on their behalf at auction at Liverpool to John Owen, Caernarvon; 1887 to H. Owen and Son, Liverpool; 1890 to Skibs A/S America (Charles Rotter), Christiania, renamed *America*; 11.1898 abandoned at sea.
Pascal (1) 1869-1897	1,950	Steamship. 1869 built by Andrew Leslie and Company, Hebburn, for Liverpool, Brazil & River Plate Steam Navigation Co. Ltd. (Lamport & Holt); 1878 to Societe de Navigation Royale Belge Sud-Americaine (Lamport & Holt), Antwerp; 1887 to Liverpool, Brazil & River Plate Steam Navigation Co. Ltd. (Lamport & Holt); 3.1897 broken up at Genoa.
Sarah J. Ellis 1869-1871	1,350	Ship. 1869 built by King, New Brunswick, for Lamport & Holt; 1871 to W. & R. Wright, Liverpool, renamed *Bride of Lorne*; 1878 to Geo. W. Gass, Liverpool; 1886 to Mrs. E. Allen, Liverpool; 4.4.1887 stranded at Pensacola Bar; sold at Public Auction to an American – no other details.
City of Rio de Janeiro 1870-1874 *Teniers* 1874-1892	1,803	Steamship. 1868 built by Randolph Elder and Company, Govan, as *City of Rio de Janeiro* for Tait and Company, London; 1870 to W.J. Lamport; 1873 to Liverpool, Brazil & River Plate Steam Navigation Co. Ltd. (Lamport & Holt); 1874 renamed *Teniers*; 1878 to Societe de Navigation Royale Belge Sud-Americaine (Lamport & Holt), Antwerp; 4.1892 broken up at Sunderland.

Name & Period in Fleet	Gross tons	History
Olbers 1870-1901	2,162	Steamship. 1870 built by Andrew Leslie and Company, Hebburn, for Liverpool, Brazil & River Plate Steam Navigation Co. Ltd. (Lamport & Holt); 1882 new engine and boiler fitted; 1886 to Societe de Navigation Royale Belge Sud-Americaine (Lamport & Holt), Antwerp; 7.1901 broken up at Genoa.
Biela (1) 1870-1900	2,182	Steamship. 1870 built by Andrew Leslie and Company, Hebburn, for Liverpool, Brazil & River Plate Steam Navigation Co. Ltd. (Lamport & Holt); 1883 new engine and boiler fitted; 1.10.1900 lost in collision with steamer *Eagle Point* off Nantucket, while on passage New York to Liverpool.
Calderon (1) 1871-1887	1,018	Steamship. 1871 built by Andrew Leslie and Company, Hebburn, for Liverpool, Brazil & River Plate Steam Navigation Co. Ltd. (Lamport & Holt); 1887 to J.N. de Vincenzi, Rio de Janeiro, renamed *Arlindo*; 1890 to Brazilian Coal Company, Rio de Janeiro, renamed *Caminha*; 1900 to A. Vianna and Company, Rio de Janeiro; 1904 to Barcellos and Moura, Rio de Janeiro, renamed *Santa Maria;* later hulked.
Camoens (1) 1871-1879	1,093	Steamship. 1871 built by Andrew Leslie and Company, Hebburn, for Liverpool, Brazil & River Plate Steam Navigation Co. Ltd. (Lamport & Holt); 1879 to W. Slimon and Company, Leith; 1888 to Navigazione Generale Italiane, Genoa, renamed *Oreto*; 1914 to Soc. anon. Vinalcool, Cagliari, renamed *Logudoro*; 1923 broken up at Palermo.
Gassendi 1872-1884	1,849	Steamship. 1872 built by Hall, Russell and Company, Aberdeen, for Liverpool, Brazil & River Plate Steam Navigation Co.Ltd. (Lamport & Holt); 1884 to T. & J. MacFarlane, Glasgow; 1886 to G. Willison, Liverpool; 1891 to G.B. Reforzo, Genoa, renamed *Madonna Della Costa*; 6.7.1894 lost by fire at Santos.
Rubens (1) 1872-1909	1,671	Steamship. 1872 built by Iliff, Mounsey and Company, Sunderland, for Liverpool, Brazil & River Plate Steam Navigation Co. Ltd. (Lamport & Holt); 1909 sold as a hulk at Punta Arenas.
Vandyck (1) 1873-1892	1,686	Steamship. 1867 built by Randolph Elder and Company, Fairfield as *City of Limerick* for Tait and Company, London; 1879 to T. & J. Harrison, Liverpool, renamed *Warrior;* 1873 to Liverpool, Brazil & River Plate Steam Navigation Co. Ltd. (Lamport & Holt), re-engined and renamed *Vandyck;* 1892 converted to a coal hulk at Rio de Janeiro.
Memling (1) 1873-1885	1,007	Steamship. 1872 built by Gourlay and Company, Dundee, as *Malaga* for Malcolm and Company, London; 1873 to Liverpool, Brazil & River Plate Steam Navigation Co. Ltd. (Lamport & Holt), renamed *Memling*; 1885 to R. Monteith and Company, Glasgow; 1886 to Raeburn and Verel; 21.1.1889 wrecked off Cape Blanco, while on passage Saffi to Casablanca.

Name & Period in Fleet	Gross tons	History
Lalande (1) 1873-1885	1,048	Steamship. 1873 built by Inglis and Company, Glasgow, for Liverpool, Brazil & River Plate Steam Navigation Co. Ltd. (Lamport & Holt); 1885 to J. MacFarlane, Glasgow; 1886 to Lalande Steamship Co. Ltd. (J. Colquhoun and Company), Glasgow; 1888 to R.D. Purvis and Company, South Shields; 1892 to Marquides Bros. and Macris Bros., Piraeus, renamed *Phoenix*; 1899 to Merli and Lugaro, Genoa, renamed *Castellaccio*; 1910 to Vassallo and Narizzano, Genoa, renamed *Bersagliere;* 1924 broken up at Genoa.
Galileo (2) 1873-1899	2,267	Steamship. 1873 built by Andrew Leslie and Company, Hebburn, for Liverpool, Brazil & River Plate Steam Navigation Co. Ltd. (Lamport & Holt); 1886 to Societe de Navigation Royale Belge Sud-Americaine (Lamport & Holt), Antwerp; 1897 to Liverpool, Brazil & River Plate Steam Navigation Co Ltd. (Lamport & Holt); 8.1899 broken up.

The *Galileo* (2) of 1873 after her transfer to the Belgian flag.   (*The Mariners Museum, Newport News.*)

Leibnitz 1873-1896	2,280	Steamship. 1873 built by Andrew Leslie and Company, Hebburn, for Liverpool, Brazil & River Plate Steam Navigation Co. Ltd. (Lamport & Holt); 1889 to Societe de Navigation Royale Belge Sud-Americaine (Lamport & Holt), Antwerp; 1896 broken up.

Name & Period in Fleet	Gross tons	History
Maraldi 1873-1875	1,002	Steamship. 1873 built by Whitehaven Shipbuilding Company, Whitehaven, for Liverpool, Brazil & River Plate Steam Navigation Co. Ltd. (Lamport & Holt); 28.2.1875 wrecked near Pernambuco, while on passage Montevideo to Antwerp.
Delambre (1) 1873-1896	1,308	Steamship. 1873 built by William Hamilton and Company, Port Glasgow, for Liverpool, Brazil & River Plate Steam Navigation Co. Ltd. (Lamport & Holt); 1896 to E. Thirkell and Company, Liverpool; 1897 broken up.
Thales 1873-1891	1,501	Steamship. 1873 built by Hall, Russell and Company, Aberdeen, for Liverpool, Brazil & River Plate Steam Navigation Co. Ltd. (Lamport & Holt); 1891 to G. Coudert and Fils, Bordeaux, renamed *Jules Coudert*; 6.1898 broken up at Genoa.
Archimedes (1) 1874-1893	1,561	Steamship. 1874 built by Hall, Russell & Company, Aberdeen, for Liverpool, Brazil & River Plate Steam Navigation Co. Ltd. (Lamport & Holt); 1893 to H. Duchon-Doris and Cie., Bordeaux, renamed *Helene*; 1900 to G. Louit, Bordeaux; 1902 to Duroto and Beraldo, Recco, renamed *Riconoscenza*; 8.3.1904 wrecked at Montana.
Cervantes (1) 1874-1884	1,131	Steamship. 1874 built by Andrew Leslie and Company, Hebburn, for Liverpool, Brazil & River Plate Steam Navigation Co. Ltd. (Lamport & Holt); 1884 to Companhia de Nav. Norte-Sul, Rio de Janeiro, renamed *Camillo*; 1895 to J.F. Carvalho, Jnr., Rio de Janeiro, renamed *Norte-Sul*; 8.1897 sank in Rio Grande del Norte, while on passage Messoro to Santos.
Maskelyne 1874-1903	2,605	Steamship. 1874 built by Andrew Leslie and Company, Hebburn, for Liverpool, Brazil & River Plate Steam Navigation Co. Ltd. (Lamport & Holt); 1889 to Societe de Navigation Royale Belge Sud-Americaine (Lamport & Holt), Antwerp; 31.1.1903 foundered in the Atlantic in position 41.35'N, 34.40'W, while on passage New Orleans to Antwerp.
Hevelius 1874-1903	2,583	Steamship. 1874 built by Andrew Leslie and Company, Hebburn, for Liverpool, Brazil & River Plate Steam Navigation Co. Ltd. (Lamport & Holt); 1889 to Societe de Navigation Royale Belge Sud-Americaine (Lamport & Holt), Antwerp; 1903 broken up.
Rosse 1875-1898	1,683	Steamship. 1875 built by Andrew Leslie and Company, Hebburn, for Liverpool, Brazil & River Plate Steam Navigation Co. Ltd. (Lamport & Holt); 1878 to Societe de Navigation Royale Belge Sud-Americaine (Lamport & Holt), Antwerp; 1887 to Liverpool, Brazil & River Plate Steam Navigation Co. Ltd. (Lamport & Holt); 1898 to Empreza Industrial Brasiliera, Rio de Janeiro; 1902 to Brazilianische Bank for Deutschland, Hamburg; 1902 broken up at Hamburg.

5. SOCIETE DE NAVIGATION ROYALE BELGE SUD-AMERICAINE, ANTWERP, AND THE ARGENTINE STEAM LIGHTER CO. LTD.

Whilst Lamport & Holt had been involved in direct sailings from Antwerp to Brazil and the River Plate since 1866 when the *Halley* made the first such sailing, in 1877 the company obtained the Belgian Government contract to carry mail from Antwerp to Brazil, Uruguay and Argentine, involving weekly sailings. The main stipulation was that the vessels serving this service should be Belgian registered, flying the Belgian flag. As a result a wholly owned subsidiary was formed in that year as 'Societe de Navigation Royale Belge Sud-Americaine,' with a headquarters at No. 1, Quai Jordaens, Antwerp. In that year the *Copernicus* (2) was registered at Antwerp, followed a year later by *Hipparchus, Horrex, Kepler, Pascal* (1), *Rosse, Teniers* and the *Tycho Brahe*. The operation of this Belgian company continued right up until 1908.

During 1884 Lamport & Holt formed a new subsidiary under the title of 'the Argentine Steam Lighter Co. Ltd.' for the purpose of operating a feeder cargo service in and around the River Plate. This company operated until about 1900 and whilst their vessels of which there were to be ten were registered at Liverpool and varied between 300/700 gross tons, they used Montevideo or Buenos Aires as their survey port. The pioneer vessel *Amadeo* which was sold in 1892 was beached in the 1930s in the Straits of Magellan at San Gregorio, where she survives to the present day.

Lamport & Holt's fleet in 1890 numbered 59 vessels amounting to 109,493 gross tons, the largest number ever to be owned by them. In later years the tonnage increased whilst the number of individual vessels decreased. As will be seen the size of vessels was to increase.

During 1896 George Holt died, having spent over fifty years engaged in the management of the business, during which he had seen it grow into one of the leading British Liner companies, and certainly had played a major part in the development of sea-borne trade with the East Coast of South America. Before his death his nephew George H. Melly, and Sidney Jones, a son of Charles W. Jones, together with Arthur Cook, joined the partnership.

FLEET LIST Part 4

Name & Period in Fleet	Gross tons	History
Canova (2) 1876-1883	1,120	Steamship. 1876 built by Andrew Leslie and Company, Hebburn, for Liverpool, Brazil & River Plate Steam Navigation Co. Ltd. (Lamport & Holt); 1883 to unknown Brazilian owners – no other details.
Euclid (1) 1877-1898	1,559	Steamship. 1877 built by Hall, Russell and Company, Aberdeen, for Liverpool, Brazil & River Plate Steam Navigation Co. Ltd. (Lamport & Holt); 1898 to Barcellon Mours and Company, Rio de Janeiro; 1903 broken up.

The *Euclid* (1)
(The Mariners Museum, Newport News.)

Name & Period in Fleet	Gross tons	History
Horrox 1877-1903	1,707	Steamship. 1877 built by T. R. Oswald, Southampton, for Liverpool, Brazil & River Plate Steam Navigation Co. Ltd. (Lamport & Holt); 1878 to Societe de Navigation Royale Belge Sud-Americaine (Lamport & Holt), Antwerp; 1887 to Liverpool, Brazil & River Plate Steam Navigation Co. Ltd. (Lamport & Holt); 1903 broken up at Naples.

The *Horrox* of 1877 seen at New York   *(The Mariners Museum, Newport News.)*

Name & Period in Fleet	Gross tons	History
Plato 1877-1892	1,675	Steamship. 1877 built by Andrew Leslie and Company, Hebburn, for Liverpool, Brazil & River Plate Steam Navigation Co. Ltd. (Lamport & Holt); 1.3.1892 foundered 160 miles off the Scilly Isles, after breaking main shaft on 29.2.1892, while on passage Liverpool to Brazil.
Pliny 1878-1882	1,671	Steamship. 1878 built by Barrow Construction Company, Barrow, for Liverpool, Brazil & River Plate Steam Navigation Co. Ltd. (Lamport & Holt); 13.5.1882 wrecked off Long Branch, New Jersey, while on passage Rio de Janeiro to New York.
Bessel 1878-1895	1,911	Steamship. 1878 built by Andrew Leslie and Company, Hebburn, for Liverpool, Brazil & River Plate Steam Navigation Co. Ltd. (Lamport & Holt); 22.6.1895 lost in collision with Wilson Line's *Hero* in the English Channel West of the Royal Sovereign Lightship, while on passage London to Brazil.

The *Pliny* shown wrecked off New Jersey in 1882.

Name & Period in Fleet	Gross tons	History
Sirius 1878-1899	2,173	Steamship. 1869 built by Andrew Leslie and Company, Hebburn, for Star Navigation Co. Ltd. (Rathbone Bros.), Liverpool; 1878 to Liverpool, Brazil & River Plate Steam Navigation Co. Ltd. (Lamport & Holt); 1882 new engine and boiler fitted; 4.1899 broken up at Genoa.
Herschel (2) 1879-1902	1,947	Steamship. 1879 built by Andrew Leslie and Company, Hebburn, for Liverpool, Brazil & River Plate Steam Navigation Co. Ltd. (Lamport & Holt); 17.11.1901 badly damaged in collision with steamer *Ardeola* in Crosby Channel, Mersey; 1902 broken up by F. Rysdijk, Hendrik-ido-Ambacht.
Lassell (1) 1879-1900	1,955	Steamship. 1879 built by Andrew Leslie and Company, Hebburn, for Liverpool, Brazil & River Plate Steam Navigation Co. Ltd. (Lamport & Holt); 1900 to McCaldin Bros. New York; 1917 to D.M.E. Jones, New York; 1920 to Union d'Enterprises Marocaines, Casablanca; 1920 to J. Castanie, Oran, renamed *Sirene*; 1924 broken up in Italy.

The first *Lassell* of 1879.

Name & Period in Fleet	Gross tons	History
Nasmyth (1) 1880-1902	1,991	Steamship. 1880 built by Andrew Leslie and Company, Hebburn, for Liverpool, Brazil & River Plate Steam Navigation Co. Ltd. (Lamport & Holt); 6.1902 broken up by Cerruti and Sons, Genoa.

The *Nasmyth* (1) held the distinction of being the first ship to berth at the new seaport of Santos on February 3, 1892.

Stella 1880-1894	106	Steam Tug. 1880 built by Liverpool Forge Company, Liverpool, for Liverpool, Brazil & River Plate Steam Navigation Co. Ltd. (Lamport & Holt); 6.7.1894 sold, no other details.
Mozart 1881-1902	1,994	Steamship. 1881 built by Andrew Leslie and Company, Hebburn, for Liverpool, Brazil & River Plate Steam Navigation Co. Ltd. (Lamport & Holt); 1902 broken up by F. Rysdijk, Hendrik-ido-Ambacht.

The *Mozart* of 1,994 gross tons dating from 1881.

Name & Period in Fleet	Gross tons	History
Strabo (1) 1881-1905	1,959	Steamship. 1881 built by Barrow Construction Company, Barrow, for Liverpool, Brazil & River Plate Steam Navigation Co. Ltd. (Lamport & Holt); 2.1905 broken up at Genoa.
Handel 1881-1902	1,977	Steamship. 1881 built by Andrew Leslie and Company, Hebburn, for Liverpool, Brazil & River Plate Steam Navigation Co. Ltd. (Lamport & Holt); 1902 to E. Malucci, Ancona, renamed *Guasco*; 1911 broken up at Cadimare.
Cavour (1) 1881-1891	618	Steamship. 1881 built by Scott and Company, Greenock, for Liverpool, Brazil & River Plate Steam Navigation Co. Ltd. (Lamport & Holt); 1891 to Lage Irmaos, Rio de Janeiro, renamed *Itapeva*; 1896 to Cia Nacional de Nav. Costeira, Rio de Janeiro; 1898 to Brazilian Lighthouse Service, renamed *Commandante Freitas*; 1930 broken up at Rio de Janeiro.
Dalton 1881-1895	2,030	Steamship. 1881 built by Andrew Leslie and Company, Hebburn, for Liverpool, Brazil & River Plate Steam Navigation Co. Ltd. (Lamport & Holt); 28.9.1895 wrecked on Isle of Islay, while on passage New York to the Clyde.
Mytilene	1,827	Steamship. 1881 built by Short Bros., Sunderland, for Lumsdon, Byers and Co. Ltd.; Lamport & Holt's records showed that they had an interest in this ship, no other details.
Ilios	2,020	Steamship. 1882 built by Short Bros., Sunderland, for Lumsdon, Byers and Co. Ltd.; Lamport & Holt's records showed that they had an interest in this ship, no other details.
Holbein (1) 1882-1901	2,050	Steamship. 1882 built by Andrew Leslie and Company, Hebburn, for Liverpool, Brazil & River Plate Steam Navigation Co. Ltd. (Lamport & Holt); 1901 to Tintore y Cia., Barcelona, renamed *Tambre*; 1905 to Linea de Vapores Tintore, Barcelona; 1916 to Cia Transmediterranea, Barcelona; 1930 broken up.
Hogarth (1) 1882-1904	2,053	Steamship. 1882 built by Andrew Leslie and Company, Hebburn, for Liverpool, Brazil & River Plate Steam Navigation Co. Ltd. (Lamport & Holt); 1904 to F. Mattarazzo and Company, Santos, renamed *Attilio*; 1922 broken up at Rio de Janeiro.

The *Hogarth* (1)

Name & Period in Fleet	Gross tons	History

Flaxman
1882-1903

2,167

Steamship. 1882 built by Oswald, Mordaunt and Company, Southampton, for Liverpool, Brazil & River Steam Navigation Co. Ltd. (Lamport & Holt); 1903 to Empreza de Nav. Salina (Rodrigues Faria and Cie), Rio de Janeiro, renamed *Canoe*; 1906 to Cia Comercio de Navegacao (Pereira Carneiro), Rio de Janeiro, renamed *Jaguaribe*; 24.8.1932 sank while on passage Rio de Janeiro to Manaos.

The *Flaxman* in the River Avon.

Chatham (1)
1883-1891

647

Steamship. 1883 built by Scott and Company, Greenock, for Liverpool, Brazil & River Plate Steam Navigation Co. Ltd. (Lamport & Holt); 1891 to Lage Irmaos, Rio de Janeiro, renamed *Itauna*; 1896 to Cia. Nacional de Nav. Costeira, Rio de Janeiro; 1931 broken up at Rio de Janeiro.

Canning (1)
1883-1891

645

Steamship. 1883 built by Scott and Company, Greenock, for Liverpool, Brazil & River Plate Steam Navigation Co. Ltd. (Lamport & Holt); 1891 to Lage Irmaos, Rio de Janeiro, renamed *Itatiaya*; 1896 to Cia. Nacional de Nav. Costeira, Rio de Janeiro; 1930 broken up at Rio de Janeiro.

Cuvier
1883-1900

2,299

Steamship. 1883 built by Andrew Leslie and Company, Hebburn, for Liverpool, Brazil & River Plate Steam Navigation Co. Ltd. (Lamport & Holt); 9.3.1900 lost in collision with the steamer *Dovre* off the East Goodwin Lightship, while on passage Antwerp to Brazil. 26 lives were lost; there were only three survivors – the officer of the watch, helmsman and lookout.

Buffon
1883-1908

2,304

Steamship. 1883 built by Andrew Leslie and Company, Hebburn, for Liverpool, Brazil & River Plate Steam Navigation Co. Ltd. (Lamport & Holt); 1908 to Cia. Comercio de Navegacao, Rio de Janeiro, renamed *Tijuca*; 20.5.1917 torpedoed and sunk off Ushant.

Amadeo
1884-1892

411

Steamship. 1884 built by Liverpool Forge Company, Liverpool, for Argentine Steam Lighter Co. Ltd. (Lamport & Holt); 1.10.1892 to J. Menendez, Punta Arenas; 1909 owners restyled as Soc. Anon. Ganadera y Comercial Menendez y Behety, Punta Arenas; 1929 Port of registry changed to Magallenes; 1930s beached in the Straits of Magellan, at San Gregorio, wreck of the ship survives at this location to this day.

The *Amadeo* of 1884 was the pioneer vessel of the Argentine Steam Lighter Co.Ltd. She is shown in the Straits of Magellen, at San Gregorio, where she has lain beached since the 1930s.
(H. Matthews)

Brenda 1884-1893	411	Steamship. 1884 built by Liverpool Forge Company, Liverpool, for Argentine Steam Lighter Co. Ltd. (Lamport & Holt); 1893 wrecked, no other details.
Caxton 1885-1895	2,687	Steamship. 1883 built by Oswald, Mordaunt and Company, Southampton, as *Test* for T.R. Oswald, Liverpool; 1885 to Liverpool, Brazil & River Plate Steam Navigation Co. Ltd. (Lamport & Holt), renamed *Caxton*; 1895 to T. Hogan and Sons, Liverpool, renamed *Mendota*; 1900 to C. Parodi, Genoa, renamed *Angiolina*; 1905 renamed *Citta di New York*; 1907 to A. Parodi fu B., Genoa, renamed *Constanza*; 1911 to G. Palazio, Genoa; 14.8.1917 torpedoed and sunk in the North Sea.
Garrick 1885-1906	2,561	Steamship. 1885 built by Andrew Leslie and Company, Hebburn, for Liverpool, Brazil & River Plate Steam Navigation Co. Ltd. (Lamport & Holt); 1906 to Acties Sandefjord Hvalfangerselskab (P. Bogan), Sandefjord, as a whaling supply ship, and renamed *Fridtjof Nansen*; 10.11.1906 wrecked at South Georgia Island.

The *Garrick* of 1885 was another product of Andrew Leslie and Company, Hebburn-on-Tyne.

Name & Period in Fleet	Gross tons	History
Spenser (1) 1885-1895	2,577	Steamship. 1885 built by Oswald, Mordaunt and Company, Southampton, for Liverpool, Brazil & River Plate Steam Navigation Co. Ltd. (Lamport & Holt); 1895 to T. Hogan and Sons, Liverpool, renamed *Manitou*; 1899 to G.B. Sturlese, Genoa, renamed *Ida*; 8.1909 broken up in Italy.
Dryden (1) 1885-1895	2,743	Steamship. 1885 built by Andrew Leslie and Company, Hebburn, for Liverpool, Brazil & River Plate Steam Navigation Co. Ltd. (Lamport & Holt); 1895 to T. Hogan and Sons, New York, renamed *Menemsha*; 1898 to United States Navy for use as a transport during Spanish American War, renamed *Iris*; 1921 to Swayne and Hoyt, San Francisco; 1928 broken up at San Francisco.
Como 1885-1889	477	Steamship. 1885 built by Barrow Shipbuilding Company, Barrow, for Argentine Steam Lighter Co. Ltd. (Lamport & Holt); 1889 wrecked, no other details.
Delta 1886-1888	289	Steamship. 1886 built by J. Jones and Sons, Liverpool, for Argentine Steam Lighter Co. Ltd. (Lamport & Holt); 4.1888 to La Platense Flotilla Co. Ltd., Glasgow; 1893 to N. Mihanovich, Buenos Aires; 1907 to P. Besana, Buenos Aires; 1917 no other details.
Elena 1886-1888	289	Steamship. 1886 built by J. Jones and Sons, Liverpool, for Argentine Steam Lighter Co. Ltd. (Lamport & Holt); 3.1888 to La Platense Flotilla Co. Ltd., Glasgow; 1892 to Brazilian Government, Rio Grande do Sul; 1907 no other details.
Chaucer (1) 1886-1913	2,769	Steamship. 1886 built by R. & W. Hawthorn, Leslie and Co. Ltd., Hebburn, for Liverpool, Brazil & River Plate Steam Navigation Co. Ltd. (Lamport & Holt); 1913 broken up by G. Longueville, Dunkirk.
Siddons (1) 1886-1894	2,846	Steamship. 1886 built by Oswald, Mordaunt and Company, Southampton, for Liverpool, Brazil & River Plate Steam Navigation Co. Ltd. (Lamport & Holt); 1894 to Bellingall and Garroway, Glasgow; 18.4.1896 lost in collision with the steamer *Craigearn* off Norderney, while on passage Odessa to Hamburg.
Copernicus (3) 1888-1895	3,230	Steamship. 1887 built by Oswald, Mordaunt and Company, Southampton, as *Lilian* for E. Bates and Sons, Liverpool; 1888 to Liverpool, Brazil & River Plate Steam Navigation Co. Ltd. (Lamport & Holt), renamed *Copernicus*; 16.10.1895 went missing on passage from Sandy Point to Valparaiso.
Newton (2) 1888-1910	2,540	Steamship. 1888 built by R. & W. Hawthorn, Leslie and Co. Ltd., Hebburn, for Liverpool, Brazil & River Plate Steam Navigation Co. Ltd. (Lamport & Holt); 1910 broken up at Antwerp.
Milton 1888-1911	2,679	Steamship. 1888 built by D. & W. Henderson and Co. Ltd., Glasgow, for Liverpool, Brazil & River Plate Steam Navigation Co. Ltd. (Lamport & Holt); 15.6.1911 wrecked off Portugal, near Cabo Espichel, while on passage London to Santos.

The *Milton* sailed from Liverpool on her maiden voyage to Buenos Aires on October 2, 1888,and when leaving the latter port in November was superficially damaged in a collision with the Lamport & Holt vessel *Archimedes*.

The *Archimedes* was seriously damaged, but re-entered service following repairs.

Freda 1888-1898	498	Steamship. 1888 built by Naval Construction and Armament Co. Ltd.,. for Argentine Steam Lighter Co. Ltd. (Lamport & Holt); 7.7.1898 sold, no other details.
Gerda 1888-1898	498	Steamship. 1888 built by Naval Construction and Armament Co. Ltd., Barrow, for Argentine Steam Lighter Co. Ltd. (Lamport & Holt); 1898 to J.G. Nogueira, Rio de Janeiro, renamed *Allianca*; 1909 to B.A. Antunes and Company, Para; 1917 no other details.
Wordsworth 1889-1902	3,260	Steamship. 1882 built by Andrew Leslie and Company, Hebburn, as *Capella* for Star Navigation Company (Rathbone Bros.), Liverpool; 1889 to Liverpool, Brazil & River Plate Steam Navigation Co. Ltd. (Lamport & Holt), renamed *Wordsworth*; 1890 to Societe de Navigation Royale Belge Sud-Americaine (Lamport & Holt), Antwerp; 1.8.1902 wrecked near Bahia, while on passage from New York.
Coleridge 1889-1904	2,610	Steamship. 1875 built by Andrew Leslie and Company, Hebburn, as *Mira* for Star Navigation Company (Rathbone Bros.), Liverpool; 1889 to Liverpool, Brazil & River Plate Steam Navigation Co. Ltd. (Lamport & Holt), renamed *Coleridge*; 1890 to Societe de Navigation Royale Belge Sud-Americaine (Lamport & Holt), Antwerp; 1890 new engine and boiler fitted; 1892 to Liverpool, Brazil & River Plate Steam Navigation Co. Ltd. (Lamport & Holt); 6.1904 broken up at Marseilles.

The *Coleridge* of 1875 was acquired from Rathbone Brothers, Liverpool, in 1889.
(National Maritime Museum)

Name & Period in Fleet	Gross tons	History
Hilda 1889-1895	537	Steamship. 1889 built by Naval Construction and Armament Co. Ltd., Barrow, for Argentine Steam Lighter Co. Ltd. (Lamport & Holt); 1895 no other details.
Ida 1889-1899	561	Steamship. 1889 built by Naval Construction and Armament Co. Ltd., Barrow, for Argentine Steam Lighter Co. Ltd. (Lamport & Holt); 3.10.1899 to N. Mihanovich, Buenos Aires; 1907 to Soc. Anon. Sud Atlantica, Buenos Aires; 1917 no other details.
Luna 1889-1894	193	Steam tug. 1889 built by Cochran and Company, Birkenhead, for Liverpool, Brazil & River Plate Steam Navigation Co. Ltd. (Lamport & Holt); 17.8.1894 to N. Mihanovich, Buenos Aires; 1907 to Nav. a Vap. Nicolas Mihanovich Ltda., Buenos Aires; 1913 to Cia. Argentina de Nav. Nicolas Mihanovich Ltda., Buenos Aires; 1923 to Cia Uruguaya de Nav. Ltda., Montevideo; 1924 registry transferred to Buenos Aires; 1933 converted to a motorship, gross tonnage increased to 237; 1942 to Cia. de Nav. Dodero (Compania de Navegacion Fluvial Argentina S.A.), Buenos Aires; c1976 beached and abandoned in the River Plate.
No. 1 *Alsina* 1889-1949	274	Lighter. 1889 built by W.H. Potter and Son, Liverpool, for Liverpool, Brazil & River Plate Steam Navigation Co. Ltd. (Lamport & Holt); later renamed *Alsina*; 1949 to Anglo Frigrifico, Buenos Aires; 22.12.1953 British registry certificate surrendered, no other details.
No. 2 *Balcarce* 1889-1930	274	Lighter. 1889 built by W.H. Potter and Son, Liverpool, for Liverpool, Brazil & River Plate Steam Navigation Co. Ltd. (Lamport & Holt), later renamed *Balcarce*; still trading in mid-1930s, no other details.
No. 3 1890-1891	274	Lighter. 1890 built by W.H. Potter and Son, Liverpool, for Liverpool, Brazil & River Plate Steam Navigation Co. Ltd. (Lamport & Holt); 1891 wrecked, no other details.
Chantrey 1890-1896	2,788	Steamship. 1890 built by R. & W. Hawthorn, Leslie and Co. Ltd., Hebburn, for Liverpool, Brazil & River Plate Steam Navigation Co. Ltd. (Lamport & Holt); 17.10.1896 wrecked near Valparaiso, on passage from Quayaquil.
Phidias (1) 1890-1911	2,822	Steamship. 1890 built by R. & W. Hawthorn, Leslie and Co. Ltd., Hebburn, for Liverpool, Brazil & River Plate Steam Navigation Co. Ltd. (Lamport & Holt); 1911 to Cia. Comercio de Navegacao, Rio de Janeiro, renamed *Tupy*; 21.9.1918 wrecked near Agadir.
Flamsteed (2) 1892-1893	3,381	Steamship. 1892 built by R. & W. Hawthorn, Leslie and Co. Ltd., Hebburn, for Liverpool, Brazil & River Plate Steam Navigation Co. Ltd. (Lamport & Holt); 26.3.1893 wrecked on coast of Chile, near Imperial River, while on passage Antwerp to Valparaiso; wreck sold and broken up as lies.

Name & Period in Fleet	Gross tons	History
Homer 1895-1912	2,585	Steamship. 1895 built by Sir Raylton Dixon and Co. Ltd., Middlesbrough, for Liverpool, Brazil & River Plate Steam Navigation Co. Ltd. (Lamport & Holt); 1912 to Urige y Egiraun, Montevideo, renamed *Odila*; 1914 registered at Bilbao; 1915 to O.F. Olsen, Bergen, renamed *Solbakken*; 4.2.1917 torpedoed and sunk off Cape Finisterre.
Horace 1895-1916	3,335	Steamship. 1895 built by D. & W. Henderson and Co. Ltd., Glasgow, for Liverpool, Brazil & River Plate Steam Navigation Co. Ltd. (Lamport & Holt); 9.2.1916 sunk by the raider *Moewe*, 600 miles North East of Pernambuco.

The *Horace* of 1895.

Name & Period in Fleet	Gross tons	History
Canova (3) 1895-1917	4,637	Steamship. 1895 built by D. & W. Henderson and Co. Ltd., Glasgow, for Liverpool, Brazil & River Plate Steam Navigation Co. Ltd. (Lamport & Holt); 1901 to Societe de Navigation Royale Belge Sud-Americaine (Lamport & Holt), Antwerp; 1908 to Liverpool, Brazil & River Plate Steam Navigation Co. Ltd. (Lamport & Holt); 24.12.1917 torpedoed and sunk 15 miles South of Mine Head, Ireland.

The *Canova* (3)

Name & Period in Fleet	Gross tons	History

Cavour (2)
1895-1929

4,978

Steamship. 1895 built by Sir Raylton Dixon and Co. Ltd., Middlesbrough, for Liverpool, Brazil & River Plate Steam Navigation Co. Ltd. (Lamport & Holt); 3.1929 to Dutch shipbreakers; 6.1929 resold and broken up at Danzig.

The *Cavour* (2) dressed overall on the occasion of a Royal visit to the Mersey in 1913. On completion in 1895, at 4,978 gross tons, she was the biggest ship to have joined the Lamport & Holt fleet.

Cervantes (2)
1895-1914

4,635

Steamship. 1895 built by D. & W. Henderson and Co. Ltd., Glasgow, for Liverpool, Brazil & River Plate Steam Navigation Co. Ltd. (Lamport & Holt); 1902 to Societe de Navigation Royale Belge Sud-Americaine (Lamport & Holt), Antwerp; 1908 to Liverpool, Brazil & River Plate Steam Navigation Co. Ltd. (Lamport & Holt); 8.10.1914 lost by enemy action with cruiser *Karlsruhe* 100 miles South West of St. Paul's Rocks.

An imposing view of the *Cervantes* (2) taking on bunkers.

(World Ship Photo Library)

Name & Period in Fleet	Gross tons	History
Juanita 1895-1899	719	Steamship. 1895 built by D. & W. Henderson and Co. Ltd., Glasgow, for Argentine Steam Lighter Co. Ltd. (Lamport & Holt); 31.10.1899 to N. Mihanovich, Buenos Aires; 1907 to Soc. Anon. Sud Atlantica, Buenos Aires; 1917 no other details.
Canning (2) 1896-1921	5,366	Steamship. 1896 built by D. & W. Henderson and Co. Ltd., Glasgow for Liverpool, Brazil & River Plate Steam Navigation Co. Ltd. (Lamport & Holt); 1914 requisitioned by the Admiralty for service as a balloon ship – HMS *Canning*; 1919 returned to Liverpool, Brazil & River Plate Steam Navigation Co. Ltd. (Lamport & Holt); 1921 to J. Vassiliou, Piraeus, renamed *Okeanis*; 1924 to Ditta Pittaluga, Genoa, renamed *Arenzano*; 1925 broken up at Genoa.

The 5,366 gross ton *Canning* (2) of 1896 which shows the increasing size of the ships joining the fleet. By now the vessels were delivered with three square sails on the foremast. In the Boer War she was employed as a transport, carrying mules from Argentina.

| *Virgil* (1)
1896-1924 | 3,338 | Steamship. 1896 built by D. & W. Henderson and Co. Ltd., Glasgow for Liverpool, Brazil & River Plate Steam Navigation Co. Ltd. (Lamport & Holt); 3.1924 broken up by Schweitzer and Oppler, Germany. |

The *Virgil* (1).

Name & Period in Fleet	Gross tons	History
Sallust (1) 1898-1924	3,628	Steamship. 1898 built by Sir Raylton Dixon and Co. Ltd., Middlesbrough, for Liverpool, Brazil & River Plate Steam Navigation Co. Ltd. (Lamport & Holt); 1924 broken up by M. Stern and Company, Hamburg.

The *Sallust* (1).
(World Ship Photo Library)

Name & Period in Fleet	Gross tons	History
Raphael (1) 1898-1930	5,855	Steamship. 1898 built by D. & W. Henderson and Co. Ltd., Glasgow for Liverpool, Brazil & River Plate Steam Navigation Co. Ltd. (Lamport & Holt); 1930 broken up by T. W. Ward, Morecambe.

The 'R' class steamer *Raphael* (1) of 5,855 gross tons was designed to carry cattle on the hoof from Argentina.
(National Maritime Museum)

Name & Period in Fleet	Gross tons	History
Romney (1) 1899-1926	4,501	Steamship. 1899 built by Sir Raylton Dixon and Co. Ltd., Middlesbrough, for Liverpool, Brazil & River Plate Steam Navigation Co. Ltd. (Lamport & Holt); 12.1926 broken up by Petersen and Albeck, Copenhagen.

The *Romney* (1) *(World Ship Photo Library)*

Rembrandt 1899-1922	4,667	Steamship. 1899 built by D. & W. Henderson and Co. Ltd., Glasgow for Liverpool, Brazil & River Plate Steam Navigation Co. Ltd. (Lamport & Holt); 3.1922 broken up in Germany.
Raeburn (1) 1900-1931	6,511	Steamship. 1900 built by D. & W. Henderson and Co. Ltd., Glasgow, for Liverpool, Brazil & River Plate Steam Navigation Co. Ltd. (Lamport & Holt); 4.1931 broken up at Savona.
Rossetti (1) 1900-1929	6,540	Steamship. 1900 built by D. & W. Henderson and Co. Ltd., Glasgow, for Liverpool, Brazil & River Plate Steam Navigation Co. Ltd. (Lamport & Holt); 1929 broken up at Danzig.
Camoens 1900-1924	4,070	Steamship. 1900 built by Workman, Clark and Co. Ltd., Belfast, for Liverpool, Brazil & River Plate Steam Navigation Co. Ltd. (Lamport & Holt); 1901 to Societe de Navigation Royale Belge Sud-Americaine (Lamport & Holt), Antwerp; 1908 to Liverpool, Brazil & River Plate Steam Navigation Co. Ltd. (Lamport & Holt); 3.1924 to Germany for scrap, but 9.1924 to A. Arditi, Genoa, for breaking up.

The *Calderon* (2) at Manchester.

Name & Period in Fleet	Gross tons	History
Calderon (2) 1900-1912	4,083	Steamship. 1900 built by Workman, Clark and Co. Ltd., Belfast, for Liverpool, Brazil & River Plate Steam Navigation Co. Ltd. (Lamport & Holt); 1901 to Societe de Navigation Royale Belge Sud-Americaine (Lamport & Holt), Antwerp; 1908 to Liverpool, Brazil & River Plate Steam Navigation Co. Ltd. (Lamport & Holt); 23.1.1912 broke in two after collision with vessel *Musketeer*, in Crosby Channel, River Mersey; total loss.
Thespis 1901-1930	4,343	Steamship. 1901 built by Sir Raylton Dixon and Co. Ltd., Middlesbrough, for Liverpool, Brazil & River Plate Steam Navigation Co. Ltd. (Lamport & Holt); 4.1930 broken up by Hughes, Bolckow and Company, Blyth.

6. EXPANSION OF PASSENGER SERVICES

In the period 1898 to 1902 twelve steamers joined the fleet, of which the five 'R' class were specifically designed to carry cattle on the hoof from Argentina to the United Kingdom, two of these were at 6,500 gross tons the largest vessels to join the fleet, ie *Raeburn* (1) and *Rossetti* (1).

Lamport & Holt had, right from the start of the entry into the South American trade with steamers in 1863, carried a significant number of saloon passengers in their cargo ships, and had been engaged to some extent in the emigrant trade from Spain and Portugal to the South American Republics, carrying large numbers of steerage passengers. However, they now saw the greatest opportunities for the carriage of passengers as being on the run between New York and South America. In 1902 the Furness Withy company had found that two of their modern steamers, the *Evangeline* and *Loyalist*, both of 3,900 gross tons, and built by A. Stephen and Son Ltd., Glasgow, in 1900 and 1901 respectively, surplus to requirements. They were quickly taken over by Lamport & Holt and renamed *Tennyson* and *Byron*. Having more than the usual Lamport & Holt accommodation for passengers they were pressed into service trading between New York and the River Plate via Brazilian ports, carrying passengers and cargo, which when Northbound usually consisted of coffee.

The *Tennyson* was one of a pair of steamers surplus to Furness, Withy's requirements, which Lamport & Holt acquired in 1902 to introduce a scheduled passenger service from New York to Brazil and the River Plate. They were both fitted to carry 70 1st, 24 2nd and 48 3rd class passengers.

This small venture into the passenger trade, helped by an ever increasing interest being paid to South America by the United States, was proving such a success, and that the company was in fact the major cargo carrier on this route, that orders were placed for the construction of three passenger liners equipped with refrigerated cargo space, and with increased speed. They were the *Velasquez* of 7,542 gross tons delivered by Sir Raylton Dixon in 1906, and the *Veronese* (7,877 gross tons) and *Verdi* (7,120 gross tons) both delivered by Workman, Clark of Belfast in 1906 and 1907 respectively. Prior to the arrival of all three ships in the fleet an order was placed with D. & W. Henderson of Glasgow for another such liner, somewhat larger, but delivered later in 1907 as the *Voltaire*.

The *Veronese* of 1906 had a gross tonnage of 7,877, but was wrecked off Portugal in 1913. (A. Duncan)

These ships quickly proved to be a great success with the travelling public, calls being made on their service between New York and the River Plate, at Salvador, Rio de Janeiro, Santos and the West Indies. They were tall elegant ships and were the best in service on that route at the time. Meanwhile the *Tennyson* and *Byron* continued to be employed from New York, but rarely went further South than Santos. It was a truly fine venture by this famous company, which had gathered an enviable reputation for itself.

However the service was not to be without incident, as on October 16, 1908, the *Velasquez* on a voyage Northbound from Buenos Aires to New York, via Brazil, ran aground on rocks between Ponta das Selas and Ponta Das Maxilhoes, near Santos, during fog and high seas. Passengers took to the lifeboats where they remained until dawn, when all were put ashore on the beach called Praia dos Vellosos. Meanwhile the *Milton*, which arrived the same day at Santos from Antwerp, was despatched to search for her, and when located on October 17, the *Velasquez* was heeled over to starboard with her stern awash. The *Milton*, not having received any response to repeated blasts on her siren, commenced a search, and it was some time later that the passengers and crew were located on the beach. All were taken on board the *Milton*, together with the mails, and she returned to the *Velasquez*, where an attempt was made to salvage the passenger's baggage. High seas did not allow completion, so the *Milton* returned to Santos on the night of October 19/20. The *Velasquez* was quickly given up as a total loss, and all attempts at salvage abandoned and attendant tugs recalled. Fortunately there were no casualties amongst the passengers and crew.

A replacement quickly appeared a year later in the form of the *Vasari* of 10,117 gross tons from Workman, Clark and Co. Ltd., Belfast, and the service was back to normal.

Of these passenger ships, the *Tennyson* and *Byron* served the company until 1922 when they were disposed of to Chile. The *Veronese* was wrecked near Leixoes, Portugal on January 16, 1913, while on passage Liverpool to Buenos Aires, via Vigo and Leixoes, in very heavy seas. Of a total of 234 passengers and crew, twenty-seven persons were lost, due in part to the terrible weather which prevented the local lifeboat from assisting in the rescue. It was only possible to rescue the passengers and crew by means of a breeches buoy after the weather had subsided somewhat. Captain C. Turner was the last to leave. The *Voltaire* and *Verdi* were casualties of the First World War, while the *Vasari* alone survived, and was sold in 1928 becoming a Fish Factory ship named *Arctic Queen*. She

The first Lamport & Holt ship over 10,000 gross tons was the *Vasari* of 1909 which was built for the New York, Brazil and River Plate service. This view before the First World War shows her at New York. *(A. Duncan)*

passed to Russia in 1935 becoming the *Pishchevaya Industriya* and finally arrived at Kaohsiung for breaking up in 1979 after a remarkable seventy years afloat. In fact, having been deleted from Lloyd's Register decades earlier through lack of information, it came as something of a surprise when she turned up at Hong Kong under her own steam en route to the breakers yard in Taiwan – for who in the West would believe that she had survived for so long.

During September, 1907 the *Raphael* struck a submerged rock off the coast of Chile, and to prevent her from sinking the master beached her, but the whole of her after deck was submerged. Eventually, after a large part of her cargo was jettisoned she was refloated a month later. Her starboard bilge had been damaged and her engines flooded. She was towed to Punta Arenas and after repairs subsequently continued her voyage to Le Havre, Swansea and Liverpool.

There was an interesting development in 1908 when Lamport & Holt took a 49% share in a 5,394 gross ton steamer, built at Le Havre by Forges and Chantiers de la Meditaranee, to the order of E. Groses, Lamport & Holt's Le Havre agent for their monthly service to the West Coast of South America, who held 51% of the shares.

The *Raphael* beached and submerged by the stern off Chile.

The *Vandyck* (2) arrived in 1911 for an intended service from Liverpool to Brazil, Uruguay and Argentina. In the event she was stationed at New York. She became a war loss in 1914.

(A. Duncan)

The 1912 built *Vauban*.

She was duly completed as the *Colbert*, for service on this route, trading under the French flag, and the company held this interest in her until her loss through enemy action in 1917.

Lamport & Holt now had four 'V' class passenger liners on the run between New York and the River Plate, and in addition the *Byron* and *Tennyson* were still serving the route as far South as Santos. Although most of the company's cargo liners trading from the United Kingdom to Brazil and the River Plate carried first class passengers and steerage passengers from Portugal and Spain Southbound, it was decided by the management to commence a similar service from Liverpool to Brazil and the River Plate. So an order was placed with Workman, Clark and Co. Ltd., Belfast, for three additional 'V' class passenger liners, which were to have twin screws. The first appeared in 1911 as the *Vandyck* of 10,237 gross tons, followed the next year by the *Vauban* and *Vestris*. The last two had slightly larger passenger accommodation than their sister, being able to carry 280 first; 130 second and 200 third-class passengers, in real luxury.

However this service from Liverpool was to last but a short time, for in 1911 the Lamport & Holt partnership had become a public company under the title of Lamport & Holt Ltd., continuing to manage the ships which remained registered under the Liverpool, Brazil and River Plate Steam Navigation Co. Ltd. Messrs. George H. Melly and Arthur Cook became joint managing directors, but the Royal Mail Steam Packet Co. Ltd was soon to take control of the company, under the chairmanship of Owen Crosby Phillips, later to become Lord Kylsant.

The *Vestris* in port. *(M. Roberts)*

Lamport & Holt became one of thirteen associate or subsidiary companies of the 'Kylsant Empire'. The following year, 1912, marked the departure of the company from Drury Buildings, Water Street, to the newly completed Royal Liver Building, on the Liverpool waterfront. Up until this time the two companies had run in competition with each other, and the appearance of three new and well found Lamport and Holt passenger liners between Liverpool and Brazil and the River Plate, did not fall in with the plans of Royal Mail at this time, who had three ships on order for their own service.

Thus it was that the Lamport & Holt ships were not to be allowed to run on this service for long. In fact while Royal Mail awaited the arrival of their new ships, two of the Lamport & Holt vessels were taken over for their own service, the *Vandyck* making only a few such voyages alongside her sister *Vauban*. The latter served Royal Mail for much longer, and was renamed *Alcala* in April, 1913, but on delivery of the new tonnage to Royal Mail, reverted back to Lamport & Holt and her original name. All three ships were then transferred to Lamport & Holt's New York to Brazil and River Plate service, with calls at Trinidad and Barbados en route, thereby leaving the United Kingdom liner trade in the hands of the Royal Mail ships. However, the loss to the United Kingdom was to be the gain of the New York service, in that the three became the crack ships on the route with their 15 knot service speed. Accounting for the loss of the *Veronese* in 1913 this left six 'V' class liners and the smaller *Byron* and *Tennyson* on the route, a truly magnificent service which was the envy of all other lines engaged in the trade. They were without doubt the most popular liners, particularly with American passengers.

Mr. Alfred C. Berry – Personal Recollections of Service at London 1910-1953

I entered the service of Lamport & Holt in September 1910 and was engaged as Dock Cashier & clerical assistant to Captain Tom P. Fisher, Marine Superintendent in London and was in his department for seventeen years. At that time Lamport & Holt had upwards of fifty vessels plying from Liverpool, Glasgow and Manchester, London and Middlesbrough to Brazil and the River Plate. They carried cement, railway material, machinery, general cargo outwards and homewards coffee from Brazil, hides and skins etc from the Argentine. These vessels were in the region of 4,500 tonnage with the exception of three small ships between 900/1,000 tons, these named *Chaucer*,

Homer and *Phidias*. From New York Lamport and Holt maintained a regular Passenger service to Brazil and the River Plate by their then famous 'V' class vessels and their tonnage was between 9,000 and 10,000 tons. Included in the fleet were several vessels which were insulated and able to carry up to 3,500 tons of frozen and chilled meat. During my earlier years with the firm, they secured a contract to carry such cargo from the Argentine for account of Messrs Weddle & Co. to London, a five year contract I believe. These ships were *Marconi, Memling, Murillo, Meissonier* and *Millais*, and discharged such cargo at 35 shed where there were special facilities for unloading. On Captain Fisher's retirement in 1927 our contract was again put out to Messrs Scruttons for outward loading.

Soon after this, the Powers that be transferred me to the London Office – 36, Lime Street, E.C. where I worked in the Cash & Passenger Dept. After a year or so our London Office was moved to Royal Mail House in Leadenhall Street and Lamport and Holt became a Limited Liability Company as we had become part of the Royal Mail Combine. One of the highlights of my career was on the day I was called into the Board Room where I found the late Mr. F.H. Lowe who informed me it had been decided to make a Freight man of me, as cargo had become hard to obtain. These were the days during the acute shipping slump in the early 1930s. It was indeed hard going in those days securing bookings in view in the intense competition then prevailing.

Subsequently we were again moved from Royal Mail House, as Lamport & Holt became separated from the Combine, a new company being formed under the title 'Lamport & Holt Line Ltd'. Soon after we left Leadenhall Street, our company went into the Cruising business with the *Vandyck* and *Voltaire*. These vessels were very popular and usually sailed from Liverpool to Madeira, other Spanish ports as well as Italian on occasion and return to UK. We had now been some years at Baltic House, Leadenhall Street, since we left the Royal Mail Group.

In 1938 I was in charge of a small party of shippers over in Antwerp for a few days. We had sailed from Middlesbrough in the *Linnell* in September of that year when rumours of impending war with Germany became ominous, and the radio news was coming through each evening when we were aboard in Antwerp. My chief in London decided to recall me to London and instructed our Agent to arrange travel facilities as soon as possible. Several of us left by the Harwich boat the same evening and arrived safely home in London the next morning. Meanwhile, as we all know Mr. Chamberlain had gone over to meet Hitler in Munich and obtained the piece of paper promising 'Peace in our time'. One year later war broke out and continued until 1945.

With the cargo position still being acute, the Conference Lines decided on a scheme whereby Shippers were required to register their bookings for cargo space with the Conference Office and when sufficient cargo warranted we took our turn to load whatever was offering.

Being fully established in Baltic House, most of the staff were fully trained as 'Fire Watchers', taking our turn on duty by rota. The raids becoming more frequent and extended over the whole country – Liverpool and Coventry having a hard time too. On Saturday 3rd May, 1940 we in London had the worst 'blitz' that evening and during the night Baltic House suffered badly. Our office was wrecked and on the Monday morning after I arrived in the vicinity of our place it was a shambles. I repaired to a Coffee House nearby where I found a few of our staff discussing the situation, when our London Manager walked in and finally arranged for us to go to a Court Line office where we could carry on meanwhile for a day or so. Eventually we learned that an empty office was available for us and in due course we were established at 85, Gracechurch Street, EC, our home when the Blue Star Line took over Lamport & Holt, and from where I retired in 1953 after forty-three years with the Company. Later the office moved and are now (1976) resident in Asia House, Lime Street, E.C. 3.

Captain Tom Edgar – Brief Personal Recollections in First World War
Was Assistant Marine Superintendent and later Marine Superintendent at Buenos Aires for 34 years

During the 1914/18 war I was 2nd Officer in the S.S. *Tintoretto* under the command of Captain W. Traunter. This was a very happy ship throughout. We were engaged carrying war materials from Quebec and Montreal to France. As *Tintoretto* was considered a fairly fast ship (13 knots) we were mostly unaccompanied as most of the Convoys were in the range of nine knots, also as we were carrying Live Ammunition we were considered 'undesirable'. During the latter part of the war we were carrying Mules from Newport News to Salonica. That also was uneventful. The only discomfort was crossing the Western Ocean light ship in the winter without a deep tank for ballast. As I mentioned before, the ship's company got on so well together we just took everything in our stride. I am pleased to say that afterwards, I was Chief Officer and Master of the 'Old Lady' *(Tintoretto)*. In later years I was appointed Master of *Strabo* on the South American trade. I was taken ashore in Buenos Aires to relieve the Assistant Marine Superintendent and later became Marine Superintendent, where I remained until my retirement, being 34 years in Buenos Aires.

Explanation regarding the Mihanovich Concern in the River Plate

The Mihanovich Co. Ltd., it owned and operated a very large flotilla of river craft both passenger and cargo with regular night passenger services to Montevideo, Corrientes and Acunsion. They also operated the principal fleet of tugs in the port of Buenos Aires and La Plata. Lamport & Holt had a large holding in this company, but I am not sure if they had the controlling interest, however, half the fleet carried the colours of Mihanovich (buff and Black) and the other half had the colours of Lamport & Holt. In the early 1930s when Lamport & Holt got into difficulties and was placed in the hands of a Receiver all the company's assets had to be liquidated and the holding, being one of the largest, was bought by Dodero & Co., chairman being Alberto Dodero. Later Dodero's was taken over by the State and remains so today (1976).

FLEET LIST Part 5

Name & Period in Fleet	Gross tons	History
Tennyson 1902-1922	3,901	Steamship. 1900 built by A. Stephen and Sons Ltd., Glasgow, as *Evangeline* for Furness, Withy and Co. Ltd., Liverpool; 1902 to Liverpool, Brazil & River Plate Steam Navigation Co. Ltd. (Lamport & Holt), renamed *Tennyson*; 1922 to Soc. Anon. Comercial Braun and Blanchard, Chile, renamed *Valparaiso*; 1932 broken up in Italy.
Byron (1) 1902-1922	3,909	Steamship. 1901 built by A. Stephen and Sons Ltd., Glasgow, as *Loyalist* for Furness, Withy and Co. Ltd., Liverpool; 1902 to Liverpool, Brazil & River Plate Steam Navigation Co. Ltd. (Lamport & Holt), renamed *Byron*; 1922 to Soc. Anon. Comercial Braun and Blanchard, Chile, renamed *Santiago*; 1932 broken up in Italy.
Terence 1902-1917	4,309	Steamship. 1902 built by D. & W. Henderson and Co. Ltd., Glasgow for Liverpool, Brazil & River Plate Steam Navigation Co. Ltd. (Lamport & Holt); 28.4.1917 torpedoed and sunk North West of Fastnet.
Titian 1902-1917	4,170	Steamship. 1902 built by Workman, Clark and Co. Ltd., Belfast, for Liverpool, Brazil & River Plate Steam Navigation Co. Ltd. (Lamport & Holt); 26.8.1917 torpedoed and sunk South East of Malta.
Tintoretto 1902-1930	4,181	Steamship. 1902 built by Workman, Clark and Co. Ltd., Belfast, for Liverpool, Brazil & River Plate Steam Navigation Co. Ltd. (Lamport & Holt); 3.1930 broken up at Savona.
Inventor 1905-1918	2,291	Steamship. 1878 built by Aitken and Mansel, Glasgow, as *Inventor* for T. & J. Harrison, Liverpool; 1905 to Liverpool, Brazil & River Plate Navigation Co. Ltd. (Lamport & Holt), carried out a loaded passage to the River Plate, and thereafter converted to a storage hulk for use at Buenos Aires; 5.1918 sold, no other details.
Velasquez 1906-1908	7,542	Steamship. 1906 built by Sir Raylton Dixon and Co. Ltd., Middlesbrough, for Liverpool, Brazil & River Plate Steam Navigation Co. Ltd. (Lamport & Holt); 16.10.1908 wrecked at Sao Sebastiano, near Santos, while on a voyage Buenos Aires to New York.

Name & Period in Fleet	Gross tons	History
Veronese 1906-1913	7,877	Steamship. 1906 built by Workman, Clark and Co. Ltd., Belfast, for Liverpool, Brazil & River Plate Steam Navigation Co. Ltd. (Lamport & Holt); 16.1.1913 wrecked near Leixoes, on a voyage Mersey to the River Plate.
Voltaire (1) 1907-1916	8,615	Steamship. 1907 built by D. & W. Henderson and Co. Ltd., Glasgow for Liverpool, Brazil & River Plate Steam Navigation Co. Ltd. (Lamport & Holt); 2.12.1916 sunk by the raider *Moewe* 650 miles West of Fastnet.
Verdi (1) 1907-1917	7,120	Steamship. 1907 built by Workman, Clark and Co. Ltd., Belfast, for Liverpool, Brazil & River Plate Steam Navigation Co. Ltd. (Lamport & Holt); 22.8.1917 torpedoed and sunk 115 miles North West of Eagle Island, Irish Sea.
Colbert 1908-1917	5,393	Steamship. 1908 built by Forges and Chantiers de la Mediteranee, Havre, for E. Groses, Havre who had 51 per cent of ship, and Liverpool, Brazil & River Plate Steam Navigation Co. Ltd. who had 49 per cent of ship; E. Groses were Lamport & Holt's Le Havre agents; vessel traded under French flag in Lamport & Holt colours; 30.4.1917 torpedoed and sunk in Mediterranean.
Vasari 1909-1928	10,117	Steamship. 1909 built by Sir Raylton Dixon and Co. Ltd., Middlesbrough, for Liverpool, Brazil & River Plate Steam Navigation Co. Ltd. (Lamport & Holt); 1928 to Hellyer Bros., Hull, converted to a Fish Factory Ship, and renamed *Arctic Queen*; 1935 to USSR, renamed *Pishchevaya Industriya*; 1979 broken up at Kaohsiung.

First World War view of the liner *Vasari*.   *(National Maritime Museum)*

The *Vasari* just prior to her sale in 1928. *(A. Duncan)*

Name & Period in Fleet	Gross tons	History
Kentmere 1909-1924	2,525	Iron Ship. 1883 built by W.H. Potter and Sons, Liverpool, for Fisher and Sprott, London; 1896 to G. Croshaw and Company, London; 1897 to F.E. Bliss, London; 1898 to Anglo-American Oil Co. Ltd. (Kentmere Sailing Ship Co. Ltd.), London, (F.E. Bliss), and converted to a four masted barque; 1909 to Pacific Steam Navigation Co. Ltd., Liverpool, for £4,500 and hulked at Punta Arenas; 6.9.1909 to Liverpool, Brazil & River Plate Steam Navigation Co. Ltd. (Lamport & Holt) for use as a storage hulk at Punta Arenas; 28.3.1924 sold, no other details.
Siddons (2) 1911-1923	4,186	Steamship. 1910 built by Armstrong, Whitworth and Co. Ltd., Newcastle, as *Tremont* for E.C. Thin and Co. Ltd., Liverpool; 1911 to Liverpool, Brazil & River Plate Steam Navigation Co. Ltd. (Lamport & Holt Ltd.), renamed *Siddons*; 1923 to R.J. Thomas, Cardiff, renamed *Cambrian Maid*; 10.1931 broken up by Hughes, Bolckow and Co. Ltd., Blyth.
Vandyck (2) 1911-1914	10,327	Steamship. 1911 built by Workman, Clark and Co. Ltd., Belfast, for Liverpool, Brazil & River Plate Steam Navigation Co. Ltd. (Lamport & Holt); 26.10.1914 sunk by the raider *Karlsruhe* 690 miles West of St. Paul's Rocks.

The *Vandyck* (2)

Name & Period in Fleet	Gross tons	History
Spenser (2) 1912-1918	4,186	Steamship. 1910 built by Armstrong, Whitworth and Co. Ltd., Newcastle, as *Tripoli* for E.C. Thin and Co. Ltd., Liverpool; 1912 to Liverpool, Brazil & River Plate Steam Navigation Co. Ltd. (Lamport & Holt Ltd.), renamed *Spenser*; 6.1.1918 torpedoed and sunk off Bardsey Island, Irish Sea.
Vauban 1912-1932	10,660	Steamship. 1912 built by Workman, Clark and Co. Ltd., Belfast, for Liverpool, Brazil & River Plate Steam Navigation Co. Ltd. (Lamport & Holt Ltd); 1913 chartered to Royal Mail Steam Packet Co. Ltd., London, renamed *Alcala*; 1913 charter ended, renamed *Vauban*; 9.1930 laid up at Southampton; 1.1932 broken up by T.W. Ward, Milford Haven.

The *Vauban* (10,660 gross tons).   (*A. Duncan*)

Name & Period in Fleet	Gross tons	History

Vestris
1912-1928

10,494

Steamship. 1912 built by Workman, Clark and Co. Ltd., Belfast, for Liverpool, Brazil & River Plate Steam Navigation Co. Ltd. (Lamport & Holt Ltd.); 12.11.1928 foundered off Virginia Cape, while on passage from New York to South America via Barbados.

The liner *Vestris* was lost in tragic circumstances in 1928.

Dryden (2)
1912-1932

5,839

Steamship. 1912 built by Wm. Hamilton and Co.Ltd., Port Glasgow, ordered by Lancashire Shipping Co. Ltd., as *Bolton Castle*, but sold on stocks to Liverpool, Brazil & River Plate Steam Navigation Co. Ltd. (Lamport & Holt Ltd.), and completed as *Dryden*; 1932 to Coumantaros Piraeus, renamed *Panagiotis Th. Coumantaros*; 1939 to J. Vassiliou, Piraeus; 1940 to S. Niarchos, Piraeus, renamed *Evgenia*; 16.5.1940 sunk by air attack off Ostend.

The *Dryden* was bought on the stocks and completed for the Liverpool, Brazil & River Plate Steam Navigation Co. Ltd. in 1912.

(A. Duncan)

Name & Period in Fleet	Gross tons	History

Archimedes (2)
1912-1932

5,364

Steamship. 1911 built by Russell and Co. Ltd., Port Glasgow, as *Den of Airlie* for Den of Airlie Co. Ltd. (C. Barrie and Son), Glasgow; 1912 to Liverpool, Brazil & River Plate Steam Navigation Co. Ltd. (Lamport & Holt Ltd.), renamed *Archimedes*; 1932 to Wm. Thompson and Company, Leith, renamed *Benmacdhui*; 10.2.1941 damaged by air attack off Yarmouth; 21.12.1941 sunk by mine 10 miles ENE of Spurn Head, while on passage from Immingham to Hong Kong.

The *Archimedes* (2) was a year old when acquired.
(National Maritime Museum)

Euclid (2)
1912-1931

4,770

Steamship. 1911 built by Northumberland Shipbuilding Co. Ltd., Newcastle, as *Horley* for Houlder, Middleton and Co. Ltd., London; 1912 to Liverpool, Brazil & River Plate Steam Navigation Co. Ltd. (Lamport & Holt Ltd.), renamed *Euclid*; 1931 to Wm. Thompson and Company, Leith, renamed *Benvannoch*; 1936 to Moller Line Ltd., Shanghai (British flag), renamed *Marie Moller*; 22.3.1937 burnt out off Holyhead, while on passage India to Liverpool, and declared a Constructive Total Loss; 1937 broken up by West of Scotland Shipbreaking Co. Ltd., Troon.

Pascal (2)
1913-1916

5,587

Steamship. 1913 built by A. McMillan and Son Ltd., Dumbarton, for Liverpool, Brazil & River Plate Steam Navigation Co. Ltd. (Lamport & Holt Ltd.); 17.12.1916 torpedoed and sunk off Casquets.

The *Pascal* (2) on trials in 1913. She was a war loss in 1916.

Name & Period in Fleet	Gross tons	History
Phidias (2) 1913-1941	5,623	Steamship. 1913 built by A. McMillan and Son Ltd., Dumbarton, for Liverpool, Brazil & River Plate Steam Navigation Co. Ltd. (Lamport & Holt Ltd.); 1934 to Lamport & Holt Line Ltd.; 8.6.1941 torpedoed and sunk by *U46* North of the Azores.

The *Phidias* (2) survived the first conflict but was lost in 1941.
(World Ship Photo Library)

Plutarch 1913-1931	5,613	Steamship. 1913 built by Russell and Co. Ltd., Port Glasgow, for Liverpool, Brazil & River Plate Steam Navigation Co. Ltd. (Lamport & Holt Ltd.); 1931 to Dubrovacka Parobrodska Plovidba, Dubrovnik, renamed *Durmitor*; 21.10.1940 captured by the raider *Atlantis* near Sunda Strait; 2.1941 retaken by HMS *Shropshire* at Mogadishu, placed under the British flag – Ministry of War Transport, renamed *Radwinter*; 1946 returned to Yugoslavia – Jugoslavenska Slobodna Plovidba, Dubrovnik, renamed *Durmitor*; 9.1963 broken up at Split.

The *Plutarch* of 1913 was sold in 1931, but survived until 1963.
(World Ship Photo Library)

Name & Period in Fleet	Gross tons	History
Socrates 1913-1930	4,979	Steamship. 1913 built by Russell and Co. Ltd., Port Glasgow, for Liverpool, Brazil & River Plate Steam Navigation Co. Ltd. (Lamport & Holt Ltd.); 1930 to D.P. Margaronis, Piraeus, renamed *P. Margaronis*; 8.3.1940 torpedoed and sunk by *U28* South West of Land's End.
Strabo (2) 1913-1932	4,930	Steamship. 1913 built by A. McMillan and Son Ltd., Dumbarton, for Liverpool, Brazil & River Plate Steam Navigation Co. Ltd. (Lamport & Holt Ltd.); 1932 to Atlanticos Steamship Co. Ltd. (Kulukundis Bros.), Syria, renamed *Pauline*; 1933 to R. Olivier, Panama; 1934 to Greek flag, renamed *Pavlina*; 1935 to Bright Navigation Co. Ltd., Panama, renamed *Brightvega*; 1936 to N.C. Wan, Shanghai, renamed *Shou Sing*; 1938 taken by the Japanese – to Yamashita K.K., renamed *Yamayuri Maru*; 24.1.1944 bombed and sunk by United States Air Force off Bougainville.

The *Strabo* (2).
(National Maritime Museum)

Anta 1913	268	Steam tug. 1912 built by Fabriech Delopthaven, Rotterdam, as *Salado II*; 6.1913 to Liverpool, Brazil & River Plate Steam Navigation Co. Ltd. (Lamport & Holt Ltd.), for £1,900 and renamed *Anta*; no other details.
Herschel (3) 1914-1934	6,293	Steamship. 1914 built by D. & W. Henderson and Co. Ltd., Glasgow, for Liverpool, Brazil & River Plate Steam Navigation Co. Ltd. (Lamport & Holt Ltd.); 1934 broken up in Italy.

The *Herschel* (3) laid up in the early 1930s.
World Ship Photo Library)

Holbein (2) 1915-1935	6,278	Steamship. 1915 built by D. & W. Henderson and Co. Ltd., Glasgow, for Liverpool, Brazil & River Plate Steam Navigation Co. Ltd. (Lamport & Holt Ltd.); 1935 broken up in Italy.

7.   THE FIRST WORLD WAR

At the outbreak of the First World War the company owned a fleet of thirty-six steamers amounting to a total gross tonnage of 198,992, and during the period of hostilities eleven of these vessels were lost through enemy action, including three of the 'V' class passenger liners. In addition the ship under the French flag, in which Lamport & Holt held a 49% interest, was also lost.

First loss was the steamer *Cervantes* which was intercepted by the German light cruiser *Karlsruhe*, 100 miles South West of St. Paul's Rocks on October 8, 1914. After removing her crew the cruiser sank the *Cervantes* with explosive charges. The company's second loss represented another victim of this German cruiser some eighteen days later on October 26, when the *Vandyck* on passage from Buenos Aires to New York with over 200 passengers, mostly United States citizens, and a full cargo, including over 1,000 tons of frozen meat, was sighted by the cruiser. The *Vandyck* tried to escape but after a chase the cruiser caught and captured her just before noon, 690 miles West of St. Paul's Rocks. The passengers and crew were placed on the steamer *Asuncion*, which had previously broken out of Santos, with many other prisoners, and sent to Para (now known as Belem) which was reached on November 1. After removing much of her cargo, particularly the frozen meat, the cruiser sank the *Vandyck* the next day.

After these losses the company's fortunes held for a while, there not being any loss during the whole of 1915. However, during that year on December 8 the *Tintoretto* was attacked by a submarine 70 miles North West from Alexandria. During the attack the submarine fired torpedoes and used gunfire but fortunately missed, and the merchant ship responded by using her own gun, which was to effectively end the action, as the submarine withdrew.

But the following year things changed, and on February 9, 1916 the *Horace* was intercepted by the German raider *Moewe*, 600 miles North East of Pernambuco, and sunk. The next casualty was the *Voltaire* which fell victim to the *Moewe* on December 2, 1916, 650 miles West of the Fastnet. Fortunately in all these losses there had been no casualties on board the merchant ships. However, later in the same month the modern steamer *Pascal* was torpedoed and sunk by a submarine off the Casquets on December 17 with the loss of two lives. The master of the *Pascal* was taken prisoner by the submarine commander and was to spend the remainder of the war incarcerated in Germany.

On March 12, 1917 the *Raphael* was chased by a submarine off Southern Ireland, but used her superior speed to outrun the enemy vessel, before an attack could be launched. The *Terence* was the next Lamport and Holt vessel to be lost to the enemy when she was torpedoed and sunk on April 18, 1917, North West of the Fastnet, with the tragic loss of one life. Two days later the French *Colbert* was torpedoed and sunk in the Mediterranean.

The *Tintoretto* had a second lucky escape, when on July 1, 1917 a submarine fired a torpedo at her in the North Atlantic which fortunately missed. A week later, on July 8, the *Plutarch* had the same good fortune when a submarine torpedo missed her off the North West of Ireland. Again the company's luck held out when on August 21 a torpedo missed the liner *Vasari* in almost the same location.

The following day the liner *Verdi* was to be less fortunate as she fell victim to a German submarine which torpedoed and sank her 115 miles North West from Eagle Island Co. Mayo, Ireland, with the sad loss of six crew. Four days later on August 26 the *Titian*, sistership of the *Terence* lost four months earlier, was torpedoed and sunk South West of Malta. The *Memling*, only delivered to the company two years previously, and a fully refrigerated ship of the 'M' class, was torpedoed by a submarine off Brest on October 3, 1917, and with assistance made port, but was so badly damaged that she was found to be beyond repair, and was declared a constructive total loss, and broken up. On November 27, the *Herschel* survived a submarine attack in the Mediterranean when the torpedo fired at her missed. The last loss suffered in 1917 was the *Canova* which was torpedoed and sunk 15 miles South of Mine Head, Ireland on December 24 during which action seven members of the crew lost their lives.

Mr. Tom Waring served in a number of Lamport and Holt ships just prior to and during the First World War, and although his service was only short it is quite interesting, and therefore I give details.

> After leaving school in 1909 I worked for a time in the Manchester Ship Canal office at Latchford Locks, and noted that Lamport and Holt had a weekly sailing from New York to Manchester. In March, 1913 I went aboard the *Thespis* at Latchford and asked Captain Ferguson for a position as ordinary seaman, but she had already signed on so I was given a letter of introduction to the marine superintendent at Liverpool, Captain Bird.
>
> On the following Saturday, March 8, I sailed in the *Raeburn* as ordinary seaman for Brazil, calling at Leixoes where 350 emigrants were picked up, and after four months and ten days paid off with the princely sum of £5.9s.0d., all of thirty bob a month.
>
> I served aboard the *Raeburn* for a further four voyages, and during the last was on board at Buenos Aires when the Great War broke out. The ship received orders to proceed to Santos where a number

of German and Austrian ships were interned, having already been loaded with coffee destined for the United States.

Having arrived at Santos we became a radio link between the cruiser H.M.S. *Glasgow* and the British Consul. The German steamers *Santa Maria* and *Cap Ortegal* came alongside us (the *Raeburn*) and transferred their cargo to our holds, and it was clear that their crews were not very happy about it. Finally the cargo from the German steamer *Hockfels* was transferred. During this time the German steamer *Asuncion* went around the anchorage taking on coal, stores and men to supply the raiders *Karlsruhe* and *Cap Trafalgar* and broke out on a Sunday night. We left for Rio de Janeiro, where cargo was taken on board from the Austrian *Laura* before proceeding via Pernambuco and Barbados to New Orleans where we arrived on October 3.

After discharge of the coffee, it had been intended that we were to be chartered to the British Government to transport horses and mules from Montreal to France; in the event these orders were changed and the ship was taken up by the French Government, and having grounded on a bank in the river while changing berths, we were towed off by the tug *W.C. Wilmot* on October 9.

Loading 900 mules and horses, we left for Bordeaux, with 75 cattlemen on board to tend the animals, arriving on October 28. This was the first cargo of horses and mules to arrive in France since the outbreak of war. A number of the crew were paid off here at their own request, and made their own way home, having been away for a fair time. As a result a part crew was signed on consisting of three French, one Japanese, one Spaniard, one American and a Swiss. I was promoted to quartermaster, and we left on November 5 for Newport News, passing and signalling St. Michaels, Azores on the 11th, arrived at Newport News on November 21.

Three days later the lamptrimmer broke his leg with the result that I was promoted to this position, the injured man being sent home on the *Raeburn's* sister *Romney*. Having loaded 910 horses we left on November 26 for Bordeaux, and after a rough passage arrived on December 10, to be diverted to La Pallice where we arrived the next day. During the passage we lost a total of fifty-two horses, which demonstrates the severity of the weather that we had encountered, and the extent to which these ships were loaded during the hostilities. On December 16 we left for Newport News, and again encountered bad weather; during December 20 we were hove to all day, losing the starboard lifeboat and accommodation ladder. On January 11, 1915 we arrived at Newport News and six days later left with 1,250 horses. On January 19, during very rough weather we lost most of the horses and pens from the foredeck.

Arriving at Bordeaux on February 5, we sailed again four days later, and after a fine passage arrived back at Newport News on February 24. On our arrival we discovered that the steamer *Anglo-Patagonian* had picked up our lifeboat which had been lost on December 20, and had feared the worst. After repairs we left again on March 14, arriving at Bordeaux on March 28. Leaving on April 1, we arrived at Newport News on April 16. After loading 1,250 horses we left on April 27 for St. Nazaire, arriving on May 11. Leaving four days later we arrived back at Newport News on June 1.

Having to wait a long time for a berth, we were informed that the next run was to Brest, hopefully to be paid off. We loaded 1,215 horses and sailed on June 30, arriving at Brest on July 14, where Captain Jardine was reluctant to pay us off. After discussions with the consul it was decided to despatch the *Raeburn* to Liverpool; sailing on July 18 we docked at Liverpool three days later, thereby ending a voyage which had lasted 14 months 10 days.

My next ship was Lamport and Holt's *Canova*. We sailed from Liverpool on August 14, 1915 for Brazil, via Lisbon, where we picked up emigrants for South America. After discharging in Brazil, the usual coffee cargo was loaded for New York, and we left, calling at the West Indies en route, discharging at Brooklyn. A large cargo was loaded, and we sailed for the United Kingdom on November 20; after encountering rough weather which necessitated heaving to for several days, we arrived in the Mersey on December 13, having been over 22 days on the passage, and it can well be imagined that there was much jubilation at Lamport and Holt's offices on our arrival at Eastham, en route to discharge at Manchester, as we had been more or less given up as lost.

My final voyage in a Lamport and Holt ship was aboard the *Siddons* from October 14, 1916 until January 6, 1917. The voyage was direct to Buenos Aires; Christmas Day 1916 being spent at Dakar waiting for a homeward convoy to form.

While engaged in the carriage of horses between the United States and France, the *Raphael*, on passage between Bordeaux and New Orleans in ballast in December 1914, was involved in the salvage of the *City of Lincoln* for which her crew were awarded salvage money.

The last loss suffered by the company during the war was the steamer *Spenser* which was torpedoed and sunk on January 6, 1918 off Bardsey Island in the Irish Sea, fortunately without loss of life. However a number of other ships were to survive enemy attacks. On January 26, 1918 the *Vestris* escaped when the torpedo aimed at her missed in the English Channel. The *Marconi* was torpedoed in the Mediterranean on February 27, with the tragic loss of two lives, but the ship remained afloat, reached port and was subsequently repaired. The *Meissonier* was shelled by a submarine West of Gibraltar on March 16, but managed to outrun the enemy vessel and escape. The *Dryden* struck a mine in the River Mersey on March 28 but managed to reach port where repairs were effected, and finally on August 27, 1918 the *Archimedes* evaded a torpedo in the English Channel.

Mr. Frank Evans served in the steamer *Herschel* for about two years during the war as a Naval Gunner, and his recollections are of interest.

I joined the *Herschel* at Liverpool early in 1917, having been sent up from Plymouth to join as a naval gunner. The ship had not been docked long, when to my utter amazement I noted on an elevated platform aft an imitation gun, made of wood by the 'Chippy'. It was removed and a 4.7in. Vickers gun was installed, and a full gun crew placed on board. The *Herschel* was evidently built for the Spanish passenger traffic because all the cabins were lettered in Spanish.

Leaving Liverpool at night we took on a full cargo of coal at Newport, Mon., for Port Said, and on joining a convoy at Avonmouth, set off for Port Said under the command of Captain Frodson. Having discharged, we moved to Alexandria where a full cargo of cotton was loaded for Boston (USA), where we arrived about three weeks later. Then light ship to Newport News where a cargo of coal was taken on board for Buenos Aires, for the Argentine Railway. I noted a large amount of German tonnage in port at Buenos Aires, due to the presence outside of the cruisers *Gloucester* and *Bristol*. We loaded a cargo of corned beef, linseed, Indian corn and hides, then crossed the River Plate to Montevideo where we completed with bagged wheat before setting out for Liverpool. On our way home we were in action with a submarine on the surface in the area of the Gulf of Mexico, and again with another in the Bay of Biscay, but fortunately survived both attacks, to arrive safely at Barry, eventually steaming round to Liverpool for discharge.

Our next voyage was under the command of Captain Carey, from Liverpool to Durban, via Suez, thence to Buenos Aires, where we stayed three weeks, leaving part loaded for Rio de Janeiro to take on bagged wheat. Thence to Bahia for completion with coffee, arriving at Liverpool after the armistice had been signed.

In the early part of the war most regular services were maintained, but towards the end it was found increasingly difficult to maintain the New York to South America service, it having to be reduced considerably.

The following figures produced by the company relate to the cargo carried by the *Archimedes* alone during the period of hostilities. She was employed throughout on carrying stores, etc., between the United Kingdom and France, and carried over 145,000 troops, 70,000 horses, 225,000 bags of mail, 12,000 vehicles, and a further 68,320 tons of stores and materials. During this period 351,000 tons of meat was carried in the company's refrigerated steamers to the armies in France and elsewhere.

As well as the 'R' class being used on carrying horses and mules across the Western Ocean to France, a number of other Lamport and Holt vessels were engaged in this service, and others were used for carrying stores for the armed forces to all theatres of the war. The *Tintoretto* was so employed on the route from Quebec and Montreal to France with such materials, and was later to be found with other units of the fleet carrying horses from Newport News to Salonica. During the whole period of the war, the *Canning* was used by the Admiralty as a balloon ship.

A number of ships joined the fleet during the war, having been built to the company's own order. There were two 'H' class ships, the *Herschel* already mentioned, and *Holbein* of 6,200 gross tons, delivered by D. and W. Henderson and Co. Ltd., Glasgow, in 1914 and 1915 respectively. However the *Herschel* was in the hands of the Admiralty from June to September, 1914.

It is interesting to note that Lamport and Holt had been carrying frozen meat since a contract was obtained to carry 230 tons a month in 1886, the first ship being fitted with refrigerated space being the *Thales* in 1887.

Six fully refrigerated ships were built for Lamport and Holt between 1915 and 1917, designated the 'M' class; they were easily recognised by their huge funnel which stood some 66 feet above the boat deck. Of these, four were sisterships in the full sense of the word, being twin-screw vessels, the *Meissonier, Murillo, Moliere* and *Marconi*. The first three came from the yard of Russell and Co. Ltd., Port Glasgow and were 7,026 gross tons, while the *Marconi* of 7,402 gross tons was delivered by Harland and Wolff Ltd., Glasgow, who also built the single screw *Millais*. The sixth, but first to enter service, was the *Memling* from A. McMillan and Co. Ltd., Dumbarton, previously mentioned as a war loss. The other five survived the war, and were employed on the frozen and chilled meat trade from the Argentine to London, a contract being signed with Weddel and Company. In 1929-30 the *Meissonier*, *Murillo* and *Moliere* were sold to H. and W. Nelson Ltd., of London, for whom they continued trading to the River Plate. All three passed to the Royal Mail fleet in 1932 together with the rest of the Nelson fleet, the latter two being renamed *Nalon* and *Nela* respectively. The *Meissonier* was renamed *Nasina* the following year, and was sold to an Italian firm two years later, she became a war loss when torpedoed and sunk by H.M.S. *Unshaken* off Brindisi on August 11, 1943. The other two continued to serve Royal Mail until the *Nalon* (ex *Murillo*) was bombed and sunk West of Ireland, while homeward bound from Cape Town on November 6, 1940. The *Nela* (ex *Moliere*) lasted until sold to be broken up in 1946 at Ghent. The *Marconi* was sold to Kaye, Son and Co. Ltd., London, in 1937, and was lost on May 21, 1941 when torpedoed and sunk South East of Cape Farewell in convoy, there being a heavy loss of life. The *Millais* was sold to the Blue Star Line in 1938, becoming their *Scottish Star*, she was torpedoed and sunk on February 20, 1941 East of Barbados, on passage Liverpool to Montevideo.

In the First World War six fully refrigerated ships of over 7,000 tons arrived in the Liverpool, Brazil and River Plate Steam Navigation Co. Ltd. fleet, built to carry large cargoes of frozen and chilled meat from Argentina. The two views of the *Meissonier* show her on charter to the Union Castle Line.

(World Ship Photo Library)

Meissonier
*(World Ship
Photo Library)*

The *Moliere* is also pictured on the Cape run for Union Castle.   *(A. Duncan)*

The *Swinburne* and *Sheridan* were the last two vessels delivered to the company during the war years; joining in 1917 they were both of 4,600 gross tons. The former became a Second World War loss, while the *Sheridan* was to stay in the fleet for some thirty years, mostly employed on the New York, Brazil and River Plate service until sold in 1947.

Lamport and Holt Ltd. was still a part of the Royal Mail Group, and in common with other members of the group had shares in a number of shipping ventures of a local nature in South America. Perhaps the most important of these was the large holding acquired in the Nicholas Mihanovich flotilla in December, 1917. This concern operated a large fleet of tugs at Buenos Aires and La Plata, and cargo and passenger services throughout the River Plate, even as far North as Asuncion in Paraguay. A number of the tugs in this fleet were painted in the Lamport and Holt funnel colours, and it is interesting to note that a tug which was in the fleet some time before these shares were acquired had the name *Lamport*. She still survived in the 1970s under different owners, but carrying the same name.

Captain B.S. Haikney
Personal Recollections Single Voyage in 1908 Sea-going Service from 1917-1940; Assistant marine Superintendent, Liverpool 1940-1955

I served on the *Veronese* as O.S. (Ordinary Seaman) in 1908 when a cargo of coffee (10,000 tons) was carried from Santos to Hamburg free of freight charge, at the time of the freight war with German companies. This ended the problem and a solution was soon negotiated.

On August 23rd, 1917 I joined the S.S. *Camoens* as 3rd Officer. She was a fast ship with a speed of 14 knots and 6,000 tons capacity. Her master – Captain J.E. Turner was a very experienced sailing ship man. This was the most critical period of the 1914-18 war, when zig-zagging in convoy was the method used to combat the submarines. With a Chief Officer aged 64 and 2nd Officer aged 62, I had a very tough time, keeping watch and attending to all signalling throughout the 24 hours, being the only officer on board who could read and answer signals from the convoy. We parted with the convoy at Dakar and continued on to the River Plate where we loaded grain, calling at Recife (Pernambuco) to complete with sugar; arriving at Liverpool to discharge on December 15th, 1917.

In January, 1918 I joined the *Tennyson* making two voyages between Manchester and New York. Light ship outwards, loaded with food stuffs homeward in convoy with about thirty ships. *Tennyson* being the guide with a Naval Commander and staff for signalling on board. I left the *Tennyson* in May, 1918.

In June, 1918 I joined the *Vestris* at Southampton as 2nd Officer remaining there until December, 1919. In August, 1918 we left New York for Le Havre with 800 nurses and stenographers on board. During the voyage an outbreak of Spanish flu put most of the passengers and crew out of action; eight of the nurses died in the epidemic and were buried at sea. After disembarking our nurses at Le Havre and discharged cargo, we proceeded to Dartmouth where we changed crew, provisioned ship and took in bunkers, for the next voyage. Early in the morning of November, 11, 1918 we sailed out of Dartmouth – passing through the entrance we received a semaphore signal from Admiralty Office Dartmouth: To Master *Vestris* – Hostilities will cease at 11am GMT today, November 11th, 1918. You will proceed on your voyage burning navigation lights, avoiding all traffic as much as possible, and cease zig-zagging. Report immediately any suspicious vessel to nearest radio station. This message caused a great deal of hat throwing jubilation throughout the ship and as we continued on our way, two German submarines, escorted by the Royal Navy passed on their way to Dartmouth, and – cause for more cheering etc. In the English Channel we had the pleasure of passing on the good tidings to passing ships we saw still zig-zagging.

Nine months later, in August, 1919 while on a voyage from New York to the River Plate for a cargo of frozen meat for the UK we discovered fire in No. 3 X bunker. After smothering the bunker as much as possible we called HMS *Dartmouth* cruising in the vicinity, and she accompanied us to St. Lucia where we landed about 600 American passengers who were housed in the army barracks, and food etc from the ship was ferried ashore four times a day, until the fire was extinguished, (which took about ten days, and afforded much merriment for both passengers and inhabitants). We were most grateful for the invaluable assistance of HMS *Dartmouth*. The passengers enjoyed the experience and we continued our voyage to the River Plate.

On May 20, 1920 I joined the T.S.S. *Moliere* as 2nd Officer. She was an 'M' class refrigerated ship, and sailed from the UK to the River Plate carrying general cargo outwards and chilled meat home, the homeward journey taking about 18 to 20 days. I made six voyages, on the last one she was chartered by the Royal Mail Line for a voyage to the Pacific where we loaded fresh fruit from Seattle, Portland Oregon and San Francisco, and canned salmon from Vancouver, returning to Liverpool and Glasgow via the Panama Canal. After discharging in Glasgow we laid up in the Gare Loch, Scotland. After a few months I asked for a relief, and on –

April 10th 1922 I joined the *Bruyere* at Manchester. On the third and my last voyage on the ship we left Liverpool on December 2nd, 1922, returning from the River Plate with a full cargo of bulk maize for Antwerp. In Lat 1 degree South our tail-end shaft snapped and carried the propeller with it. For three days we were helpless until we were picked up by the *Sallust* (Lamport and Holt), and towed into Pernambuco by anchor cable. I was in charge of the boat during this incident, there was a heavy swell on and most of the boat crew became helpless with seasickness. Sharks were all around the boat and biting at the oars, making the operation very hazardous. Our stay in Pernambuco was interesting, for there were no engineers in the port who knew anything about propellers, so we had to do the job ourselves with the help of shore lifting gear lent by the Sugar Engineers. The *Bruyere* on arrival had a draft of 25ft aft and 24ft forward. We had to get a draft of 8ft aft and 41ft forward, by discharging No. 4 and No. 5 holds ashore and filling the forward ballast tanks. In order to discharge the bulk maize we had to erect bins in the sheds , this took up a lot of time. Eventually the spare propeller was joined to the spare tail-end, (Every ship carries these spares), by the Chief Officer and 2nd Engineer. We then proceeded to reload the ship's cargo. This whole operation lasted about ten days. We resumed our voyage to Antwerp calling at Las Palmas for bunkers. Arriving at Antwerp in Mid-April, we discharged and sailed in ballast to Middlesbrough where the voyage ended on May, 8th 1923.

After receiving my Master's Certificate I joined the T.S.S. *Vandyck* in New York as 2nd Officer on August 4th 1923. Sailing between New York, Barbados, Rio de Janeiro, Santos and Buenos Aires. The *Vandyck* was a first class passenger ship, with refrigerated holds, and accommodation for 275 first class, 110 second class, and 500 steerage passengers. She was a very popular ship with the American passengers. When Shackleton the Arctic explorer was aboard – he was very popular with them too. We carried Madam Pavlova and her Corps-de-Ballet from New York to Buenos Aires on another voyage. On my fourth voyage which left New York on July 26th 1924 I was promoted to First Officer, making the voyage to Rio de Janeiro, where I transferred to the *Plutarch* as Chief Officer. The Chief Officer of the *Plutarch* being senior in the Company to me took over the *Vandyck*. After making three uneventful voyages in the *Plutarch* (though it took me many days to get used to the food), I was appointed to the *Meissonier* at London.

On September 9, 1925 I joined the T.S.S. *Meissonier* at London as Chief Officer being on charter to Blue Star Line, together with *Marconi*, *Murillo*, *Moliere* and *Millais*. We usually carried coal in bunker X to be emptied and cleaned before arriving at the River Plate to load chilled meat for West India Dock, London. On November 15, 1927 during my tenth voyage in the vessel I was put ashore in Buenos Aires and treated at the British Hospital for Diabetes. After six weeks in hospital I returned to the UK as a passenger on Lamport & Holt's *Hogarth*, arriving Liverpool February 13, 1928. During convalescence I served on several ships (coasting). When I eventually received a clean bill of health from the specialist I was appointed as Chief Officer of the *Balfe*.

I sailed from Liverpool on the *Balfe* on May 11, 1929 bound for South America, thereafter we made several voyages to New York and back again to Santos and Buenos Aires carrying general cargo. Returning to the UK in May, 1930. Stayed on the *Balfe*, and on my ninth which began on January 4, 1932 we fractured our rudder stock due to very heavy weather in the Bay of Biscay. The weather was so bad it was five days before we could fit a jury rudder. On the sixth day I put two men lashed to Bosun's chairs over the stern and with great courage they managed to put strops around the top rudder stock, attached these to No. 5 derricks which we lashed to starboard and port bulwarks using topping lifts to winch in reverse positions. This method enabled us to steer the *Balfe* into Lisbon under her own power. Limping into Lisbon, we were greeted by the sirens of the ships in the harbour. We tied up alongside for repairs and sailed about two weeks later, completing our voyage to the River Plate, returning to Liverpool in May, 1932.

This was the time of recession, the *Balfe* was laid up in the Blackwater River, Essex, with myself, a 2nd Officer and Chief Engineer on board. My wife and two daughters joined me. After three months I received a cheque from the Insurance Company for £38, this princely sum was apparently in recognition of my efforts on getting into Lisbon. We remained rusticating on half pay for 2½ years, but when my eldest daughter was five years old and ready for school I asked to be relieved.

I joined the *Lassell* in November, 1934 as 2nd Officer. During this depression, which seemed never ending, young officers even served as crew. Gradually conditions improved and after five voyages I reverted to Chief Officer. Thereafter I made two voyages on *Bonheur* from August 28, 1936 and from January 5, 1938 on the *Bruyere* for one. These voyages were particularly long involving intermediate passages to New York from Brazil and the River Plate.

I sailed from Liverpool on September 30, 1938 on the *Delambre* to Brazil and the River Plate returning on December 22 the same year.

Thereafter I was sent out passenger to New York, where on February 17, 1939 I joined the *Sheridan* as Chief Officer, trading between North Brazil and New York, carrying general cargo outwards, and rubber, Brazil nuts, wax and coffee back to New York.

On my second voyage when we were about fourteen days out of New York, the master – Captain Norman (aged 62) fell 16 feet from the boat deck to the after well deck fracturing his skull and other serious injuries. I asked for and received advice from the U.S. Maritime Hospital at Washington – they told me to make for the nearest port, for hospitalisation, the nearest was St. Kitts, West Indies – but tragically he died in the night. The Brazilian crew were very upset, and asked permission to keep a vigil until he was buried next day. He was buried at sea the next morning. I took over command and we continued on our voyage to Para, North Brazil, where I saw the British Consul and was put on the register. We continued our voyage up the River Amazon to Manaos. This was in competition with Booth Line, a sort of reprisal for their encroachment on some of Lamport Holt's trade in South America. It was my first trip to Manaos and to me, breathtaking, different from anything I'd experienced before – the exotic birds, the lush forests, the crocodiles, and mud hut villages with natives almost naked, everything was very primitive. On the return voyage to New York, I surprised the Agents by arriving about two days early, for the *Sheridan* was a slow ship. But I took advantage of the equatorial currents. On arrival at New York, which was the end of July, 1939, a more senior officer was waiting to take command. We sailed on July 31, 1939 for Brazil and the River Plate, and back to New York in November, 1939. Happily we had not seen any action. November 22 we left New York for Brazil and the River Plate then to Liverpool, eventually joining a homeward convoy. The *Sheridan* was so slow we could not keep up with the convoy and several times a destroyer came searching for us, urging us to get a move on, but nobody could get another ounce of steam out of her, so we had to make our own way. We arrived at Liverpool about twelve hours after the convoy. I think the Germans suspected we were a decoy. The voyage ended on March 10, 1940.

After being paid off I was posted ashore in Liverpool as Assistant Marine Superintendent under Captain S.S. Richardson RD RNR. We kept very busy with our own ships and our quota of vessels Sea Transport gave us to look after. With the Channel ports virtually closed, and our own share of air raids, life was always on the move, never a dull moment. When the United States came into the war, Lamport & Holt were the Agents for the U.S. Administration of Merchant Shipping at Liverpool. We often had twelve to fourteen 'Liberty' ships to look after as well as our own, also all docking and un-dockings.

In 1944 Lamport & Holt were taken over by the Vestey Group, but we continued to operate a big fleet. I retained my position until my retirement in June, 1955.

FLEET LIST Part 6

Name & Period in Fleet	Gross tons	History
Memling (2) 1915-1917	7,307	Steamship. 1915 built by A. McMillan and Son Ltd., Dumbarton, for Liverpool, Brazil & River Plate Steam Navigation Co. Ltd. (Lamport & Holt Ltd.); 3.10.1917 torpedoed and damaged off Brest, declared a Constructive Total Loss, and broken up.
Meissonier 1915-1930	7,206	Steamship. 1915 built by Russell and Co. Ltd., Port Glasgow, for Liverpool, Brazil & River Plate Steam Navigation Co. Ltd. (Lamport & Holt Ltd.); 1930 to H. & W. Nelson Ltd., London; 1932 to Royal Mail Lines, London, 1933 renamed *Nasina;* 1935 to Societa Anonima Cooperativa di Nav. Garibaldi, Genoa, renamed *Asmara*; 1940 to Italian Navy as a transport; 11.8.1943 torpedoed and sunk by HMS *Unshaken* off Brindidi.

The *Meissonier.* (A. Duncan)

Murillo (1) 1915-1930	7,206	Steamship. 1915 built by Russell and Co. Ltd., Port Glasgow, for Liverpool, Brazil & River Plate Steam Navigation Co. Ltd. (Lamport & Holt Ltd.); 1930 to H. & W. Nelson Ltd., London; 1932 to Royal Mail Lines, London, renamed *Nalon*; 6.11.1940 bombed and sunk by aircraft West of Ireland, while homeward bound from Cape Town.

Name & Period in Fleet	Gross tons	History
Moliere 1916-1929	7,206	Steamship. 1916 built by Russell and Co. Ltd., Port Glasgow, for Liverpool, Brazil & River Plate Steam Navigation Co. Ltd. (Lamport & Holt Ltd.); 1929 to H. & W. Nelson., London; 1932 to Royal Mail Lines, London renamed *Nela;* 1.1946 broken up by Van Heyghen Freres, Ghent.

Moliere of 1916.
  (World Ship Photo Library)

Marconi 1917-1937	7,402	Steamship. 1917 built by Harland & Wolff Ltd., Glasgow, for Liverpool, Brazil & River Plate Steam Navigation Co. Ltd. (Lamport & Holt Ltd.); 1934 to Lamport & Holt Line Ltd.; 1937 to Marconi Steamship Co. Ltd. (Kaye, Son and Co. Ltd.) London; 21.5.1941 torpedoed and sunk by *U109* South East of Cape Farewell.

The *Marconi.*   *(National Maritime Museum)*

Name & Period in Fleet	Gross tons	History

Millais (1)
1917-1938

7,224

Steamship. 1917 built by Harland & Wolff Ltd., Glasgow, for Liverpool, Brazil & River Plate Steam Navigation Co. Ltd. (Lamport & Holt Ltd.); 1934 to Lamport & Holt Line Ltd.; 1938 to Blue Star Line Ltd., London, renamed *Scottish Star*; 20.2.1942 torpedoed and sunk by Italian submarine *Torelli* East of Barbados, while on passage Liverpool to Montevideo.

The *Millais* of 1917.
(A. Duncan)

Swinburne
1917-1941

4,659

Steamship. 1917 built by A. McMillan and Son Ltd., Dumbarton, for Liverpool, Brazil & River Plate Steam Navigation Co. Ltd. (Lamport & Holt Ltd.); 1934 to Lamport & Holt Line Ltd.; 26.2.1941 bombed by aircraft West of Ireland; torpedoed and sunk by escort.

Sheridan (1)
1917-1947

4,665

Steamship. 1917 built by A. McMillan and Son Ltd., Dumbarton, for Liverpool, Brazil & River Plate Steam Navigation Co. Ltd. (Lamport & Holt Ltd.); 1934 to Lamport & Holt Line Ltd.; 1947 to Alexandria Navigation Co. Ltd., renamed *Star of Cairo*; 1950 to Transoceanic Steamship Company, Karachi, renamed *Ocean Endeavour*; 1963 broken up at Gadani Beach.

A First World War view of the steamer *Sheridan* (1) of 1917. This ship was described in the later conflict as 'the oldest, slowest and luckiest ship in the fleet'.

8. THE DEPRESSION AND LAMPORT & HOLT LINE LTD.

After the war the company began to acquire new tonnage, principally ships of the standard types built towards the end of hostilities, a large number of which had been managed by the company on behalf of the Shipping Controller. These were to fall into three classes. Two steamers of 6,500 gross tons ordered by the Shipping Controller were completed for Lamport & Holt as the *Nasmyth* and *Newton*. A Japanese built steamer of 7,000 gross tons built in 1917 became the *Delambre*. Whilst nine standard ships of 5,300 gross tons each were acquired during 1919 and 1920, some straight from the builders, others having helped in the war effort; they became the 'B' class and were named *Bernini*, *Boswell*, *Balfe*, *Biela*, *Bruyere*, *Bronte*, *Balzac*, *Browning* and *Bonheur*.

Having acquired twelve steamers from the Shipping Controller the fleet was more like its former size, but it was also felt that a new class should be laid down to its own order, and in consequence two steamers were delivered, designated the 'L' class. They were the *Laplace* and *Lalande*, of about 7,000 gross tons, delivered in 1919 and 1920 respectively, from the yards of A. McMillan and Sons, Ltd., Dumbarton, and D. & W. Henderson and Co. Ltd., Glasgow. Having taken delivery of these two 'L' class steamers, the company, ever looking to make improvements, placed an order for three twin-screw motorships with McMillan's yard. They were the first such ships to be ordered by the company and were of the same tonnage and basic appearance as the previous two steamers. The *Linnell* and *Leighton* joined the fleet in 1921, followed a year later by the *Lassell*. They proved highly successful in service. 1921 also saw the arrival of an 8,100 gross ton steamer *Hogarth*.

The *Linnell* was one of a trio of motorships which joined the Lamport & Holt fleet in 1921-22.   (*A. Duncan*)

On the passenger liner side, the old faithfuls, *Tennyson* and *Byron* both survived the war, together with the *Vasari*, *Vauban* and *Vestris*. The latter three resumed their service from New York in 1919, but initially they commenced a charter to Cunard taking passengers and cargo Westbound from Liverpool to New York, and then for their owners account going South to Buenos Aires with passengers and cargo, and returning to the United Kingdom with frozen meat from the River Plate. After about six Atlantic crossings for Cunard they resumed their service back and forth from New York to the River Plate, via Brazil, Barbados and Trinidad. In 1922 the *Vauban* and *Vestris* together with the later *Vandyck*, made a single Westbound crossing from Hamburg to New York on

Charter to Royal Mail, but after this they resumed their normal sailings.

Having lost three 'V' class passenger liners in the war, there was a gap which Lamport & Holt had to fill, and as a result they ordered two twin-screw steamers from the Belfast yard of Workman, Clark and Co. Ltd. The first of these, the *Vandyck* of 13,233 gross tons, was launched on February 24, 1921, and had five holds for refrigerated and general cargo, and accommodation for 300 first, 150 second and 230 third class passengers. The first class comprised one, two and three berth cabins, and included a number of special cabins with private bathroom, toilet and extra storage space. Her sistership. *Voltaire* of 13,248 gross tons, was launched on August, 14, 1923, and joined the fleet later that year. The *Tennyson* and *Bryon*, now somewhat surplus to requirements, and somewhat aged, were disposed of, and with the arrival of the *Voltaire*, the passenger fleet trading from New York was brought up to five ships, thereby allowing a fortnightly service on the route. The two new ships proved to be very popular with passengers, and so they ought, providing, as they did, a new standard in accommodation.

The *Vandyck* (3) of 13,233 gross tons entered service from New York in 1921.
(National Maritime Museum)

The Liner *Voltaire* (2) of 1923.
(National Maritime Museum)

On October 25, 1927 the *Rossetti* under the command of Captain W. Denson, who had joined the company in1908, went to the assistance of the *Principessa Mafalda*, which was in distress off the Brazilian coast, and when this ship sank assisted in the rescue of passengers and crew, for which Captain Denson received a Gold Medal from the Italian Chamber of Commerce. During the following year the *Vasari* was sold.

On November 10, 1928, the *Vestris*, having left New York for Barbados and Buenos Aires under the command of Captain W.J. Carey with 129 passengers and 197 crew, encountered heavy weather the next day, and on the evening of that day was struck by waves of exceptional size and force, flooding the boat deck, and amongst other damage washed two lifeboats away. Part of her cargo and bunker coal shifted, and as a result she took on a heavy lift to starboard, from which she was unable to recover, the pumps being unable to cope. By the following day the ship was in a bad way, and having failed to right her Captain Carey sent out a distress message. The ship quickly increased her list, and had to be abandoned about 300 miles off Hampton Roads, sinking at 2pm. Lifeboats were picked up by the steamers *American Shipper*, *Miriam* and *Berlin*, and by the United States battleship *Wyoming*. Captain Carey was among the 112 passengers and crew lost.

After this tragedy, a fair amount of adverse publicity was encountered, and, with the depression fast setting in, the service from New York by the passenger liners was discontinued, and the three remaining ships were brought home to be laid-up, the *Vauban* and *Vandyck* at Southampton and the *Voltaire* in the River Blackwater.

The recession was now upon the world, and to add to this the 'Kylsant Empire' became enmeshed in a complete financial crash. As a result Lamport & Holt Ltd was placed in the hands of a Receiver, who tried to save as much as possible of its assets.

In January, 1930 Lamport & Holt owned a fleet of 41 ships, of which three were passenger liners. Gradually as the depression got worse and the amount of cargo available for shipment got less, the majority of the fleet was sent to lay-up berths on their arrival back in the United Kingdom. Of these 41 ships, almost half were disposed of

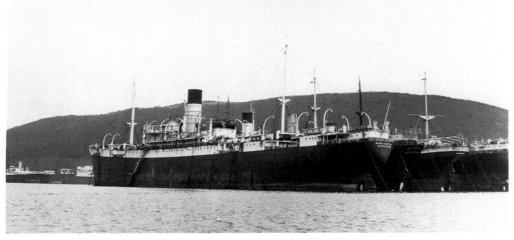

Two views of the *Hogarth* (3) laid up in the depression on the outside of a tier of ships, the nearest being *Browning* (1).
(World Ship Photo Library)

(& National Maritime Museum)

Two views of the *Balzac* (1) laid up.
(National Maritime Museum &
World Ship Photo Library)

The laid up *Herschel* of
1914.   *(A. Duncan)*

between 1930 and 1935. Considering the size of the fleet prior to the 'Kylsant Crash', and the large number of men who had been dependant on the company for a livelihood, it was a further tragedy in itself, as suddenly men who had been with them for years were now unemployed, or forced to be demoted. Masters were sailing as chief officers or even lower ranks. It was a sorry state indeed and, in an effort to improve matters for these men, the company fitted out the motorship *Lassell* to be wholly manned by officers and engineers, this in an effort to keep loyal men until better times. It was not unusual to see men qualified as master and chief engineer sailing as ratings, and this situation was by no means confined to Lamport & Holt, but was widespread at that time.

During the spring of 1932 the *Voltaire and Vandyck* were brought out of lay-up, and were made ready for a series of cruises from Southampton and Liverpool, and these proved so successful that they were specially fitted for this purpose. Their hulls were painted white, and from then until just before the Second World War they were so employed, cruising to the Mediterranean, Atlantic Islands, West African ports, West Indies, Norwegian Fjords and Baltic ports. It was at this time, in recognition of the trade and employment brought by the company to the Port of Liverpool, that Lamport & Holt were presented with the City of Liverpool's colours, and for the rest of its existence was the only shipping company privileged to fly the Liverpool Civic Flag at the jackstaff of its ships when moored in any port in the world. Whilst Lamport & Holt's funnel colours had always been blue with a black top divided by a white band; the blue had been a pale shade similar to the Argentine flag, however this shade was now changed to the darker blue, similar to the Liverpool civic colours.

The General Manager from 1924 to 1930 had been Mr. Alfred Woods, but in 1930 he was succeeded by Mr. Francis H. Lowe, who was to manage the company through its most difficult period, during the Receivership. In the middle of 1934, the Liverpool, Brazil and River Plate Steam Navigation Co. Ltd. took over all the assets of Lamport & Holt Ltd., and was reborn under the new title of 'Lamport & Holt Line Limited'. A new board of directors was formed as follows: Philip Edward Haldin (Chairman), Alfred Woods (Deputy Chairman), Francis Hugh Lowe (Managing Director), Philip Runciman, Charles Frederick Holland and William Alexander Young.

The *Vandyck* (3) in 1930s cruising livery.   *(A. Duncan)*

The majestic *Voltaire* (2) in the Mersey.   *(Stewart Bale Ltd)*

It will be remembered that the last ship to enter the fleet was the passenger liner *Voltaire* in 1923, but that the last cargo ships acquired were the trio of motorships in 1921/22. Such was the company's fortunes under the new board of directors, that in 1937 the first of an order for three new motorships appeared from the Belfast yard of Harland and Wolff Ltd., and became the 'D' class , causing quite a stir in shipping circles when they appeared due to their revolutionary profile. They were streamlined, and something of a departure from the normal appearance of a cargo liner. The funnel was incorporated into the superstructure, and housed a small part of the accommodation. Like the 'L' class before them, they were fitted for carrying twelve passengers in comfortable accommodation, and were originally designed for the company's route from Liverpool and Glasgow to the River Plate. The first ship was the *Delius*, followed in 1938 by the *Delane* and *Devis*, all open shelter deck vessels of some 6,000 gross tons. They were fitted with a double-acting 6-cylinder two-stroke oil engine built and installed by the builders.

The newly completed *Delius* in 1937. A revolutionary profile.   *(Harland & Wolff Ltd.)*

The *Delane*.   *(National Maritime Museum)*

The 1938 *Devis* (1) became a war loss in 1943.

(Harland & Wolff Ltd.)

Captain D.C. Roberts
Personal Recollections of Service 1915-1956

I was born on Christmas Day, 1890 and first went to sea in August, 1906 in sailing ships. Passed for 2nd Mate August, 1911 and went 2nd Mate of the full rigged ship *Inveravon*. Passed for Extra Master Square Rigged August, 1914. Joined Lamport & Holt in March, 1915 as 2nd Officer of the *Pascal*, and served as officer in the following ships, *Vestris, Sheridan, Holbein, Murillo* and *Laplace*.

Appointed Master of the *Raphael* in May, 1925. Her former master died at the British Hospital in Buenos Aires soon after. On arrival home I was appointed master of the *Phidias*, then in turn, the *Biela, Swinburne* and *Bruyere*, and on arrival home in the latter, the collapse of the Royal Mail Group had occurred. I then had to revert to Chief Officer as the fleet was much reduced.

It was a few months before the outbreak of war in 1939 that I was re-appointed master. This time to the *Sheridan* which I joined at New York. War broke out a few days before we arrived at Pernambuco. After arrival home from that voyage, I made two more voyages to South America in the *Sheridan*. The *Sheridan* was the oldest, slowest and luckiest ship in the fleet. On one occasion in the North Sea a German plane dropped a bomb that close, that it caused a leak in one of the double bottom tanks, we managed to carry on, but had to drydock at Montevideo. On another occasion, in a homeward convoy from Freetown, S.L., a submarine surfaced only a few yards away at night time, he fired his torpedo, missed us but got another ship in the convoy, we had taken avoiding action in time. The *Sheridan* remained in the company's service throughout the war, and was eventually sold to Egypt.

From the *Sheridan* I was appointed master of the *Debrett* for a return voyage to South America. After the voyage in the *Debrett* I was appointed to the *Lalande*, and made a voyage to the Middle East round the Cape of Good Hope then to Brazil and home. Again to the *Debrett* and to the Middle East round the Cape, stayed in the Mediterranean most of 1943 based at Port Said. After arrival home I was appointed to the *Samarovsk* went North about to London where we loaded and awaited the invasion of Normandy.

I received an OBE in June, 1945 and retired on 1st April, 1956.

Captain B.M. Metcalfe
Personal Recollections of Service 1924-1970

Aged 17 years, in May, 1924 joined *Holbein* for one voyage as O.S. (Ordinary Seaman). Carried Spanish and Portuguese emigrants. Then followed in 1925 – two voyages in the *Sheridan*, a wartime built ship, and one in the *Rossetti*. A flush deck ship, her decks timber sheathed fore and aft, and two tween decks built purposely for carrying cattle on the hoof. Hatch coamings practically flush with the main deck, wooden hatch beams and combing pieces thrown in. Wooden derricks, old type stock anchors which had to be called in and out, arriving and leaving port. Donkey boiler in No. 4 Upper Tween Deck. Cattlemen aft crew forward. Over-run by rats nesting all over the ship. Every time steam was put on the winches there followed a real scattering of rats jumping out from the winch cylinders and pipe casings to escape from a roasting. Common practice in those days to keep a supply of grain in the baggage and mail locker, in an effort to discourage rats from gnawing the mail.

In the year 1926 made two voyages in the *Herschel* – Captain Carey in command, who was in command of *Vestris* when she sank, he being lost. Then followed several voyages in the *Hogarth* commencing in the latter part of 1926. A turbine steamer and since the National Strike was on she was converted from coal to oil burning, but reverted back to coal after my first voyage. Captain Frodsham and Captain Turner in command. In early 1927 was promoted to sailor (equivalent to EDH – Efficient Deck Hand), and to Quartermaster. In those days promotion was gained only by ones ability and bloody hard work. 4 hours on and 4 off. No morning or afternoon tea breaks, in any case rations didn't allow for it. Discipline was strict, in consequence she was a happy ship in spite of all this. Her crew throughout all departments with the exception of a very few cases never changed. Carried Spanish and Portuguese emigrants, deck and 3rd class. Capacity around 500 – Portuguese forward, Spanish aft. I left *Hogarth* on completion of four years sea service, 1929 or early 1930 attended B.V. Nautical School, principal Captain Beatty (cousin of Admiral Beatty). In the six weeks that followed obtained lifeboat and ambulance certificates, sat and passed my 2nd Mates exams.

After a brief spell at home in Cumberland received word from the Superintendent – Captain Richardson to be prepared at short notice to go out as Cadet in a home ship to join one of our New York/South America vessels as 3rd Officer, which was the company's practice. Unfortunately the slump was fast settling down, ships laid-up, officers and men out of work, accordingly received a letter of regret from the superintendent informing me his offer for the post of Cadet and 3rd Officer was no longer possible. He offered me an A.B.s post in the *Holbein* which I accepted gladly. Jobs were very hard to come by.

During the period that followed I sailed with quite a number of A.B.s having Master Mariner's Certificates. I did two voyages in *Holbein*. It was then decided by the company, owing to large number of Captains and Officers being unemployed, to make an effort to keep them until times improved. Before the depression I think there were 54 ships in the fleet, now more than half laid-up or sold. In consequence the M.V. *Lassell* was chosen to be completely manned by the company's out of work officers. Deck Department all officers of all ranks – 3rd Officer to Captain, Engineroom Department 4th Engineer to 2nd Engineer, most held Master Mariners or Chief Engineers Certificates. I think it was early in 1931 when we sailed. The voyage to South America; on leaving the River Plate for home, one man went sick, then another, then myself, and in a couple of days twelve men were down, which turned out to be Typhoid. We called into Dakar for fuel and the French doctors examined the sick, prescribed and supplied medicines; and took the two worst cases ashore to hospital, where they both died. Being very short manned it was only natural as soon as our temperatures fell to normal we had to take the wheel. I recall I took the ship into Liverpool. From a hefty lad of 12½ stones, I arrived home at 7½ stone. Needless to say I convalesced for a few weeks, therefore did not rejoin the *Lassell*.

During all this time I wrote to many companies seeking employment, but to no avail; times were indeed very grim.

I think it was early summer 1931 that I was sent for by the superintendent, to stand-by as Quartermaster on the T.S.S. *Voltaire* which was being fitted out for cruising, and sailed on her first cruise as Q.M. On her return to Liverpool I was informed I was to be appointed 3rd Officer of the *Sheridan*. Went out to New York on *Majestic* to join her; she was on the New York/South America run, and never came home. Instead of doing two years out there, three passed before I was relieved. Came home as 3rd Officer from Buenos Aires in the *Lalande* in 1934.

Sat and passed First Mates exam, then one voyage in *Phidias* as 3rd Officer. Then I joined Bronte as 3rd Officer, from which vessel I transferred again to *Sheridan* in Rio de Janeiro as 2nd Officer. I served two years on the New York/South America service, was relieved and came home as passenger on *Laconia* in December, 1937.

Early in 1938 I attended Liverpool Tech. and in April sat and passed my Master's exam. Joined the *Vandyck* as Launch Officer for one Norwegian cruise, then transferred to *Voltaire* as 2nd Officer on Northern Capital and Mediterranean cruises. These continued until the Spring of 1939 when all cruising ceased owing to the threat of hostilities. She was then converted to carrying troops. Sailed for Bombay in June with troops. On way home with NCOs and their families, when in the Bay of Biscay received Admiralty A Message – War was imminent. Arrived in Southampton August 28, 1939. That night ship was painted battleship grey. No one allowed ashore. Following evening sailed for Scapa Flow.

Author's Note: Captain Metcalfe's war service onboard *Voltaire* appears in the chapter on the hostilities later in this volume.

Towards the end of 1940, a fleet order was issued, in effect that the Admiralty would like all officers (T124) personnel, holding Master's Certificates to become pukker RNR until the end of hostilities, if they wished. I along with three or four colleagues decided not to, and to revert back to the Merchant Service. I left *Voltaire* in Halifax, she then sailed for Trinidad to fuel before proceeding on to Freetown to escort convoys. It was on this passage from Trinidad that the *Voltaire* was sunk by a German raider. In the meantime I was on the M.V. *British Prince* bound for Liverpool Bay.

Berthed in Manchester early Good Friday morning 1941 and reported to HMS *Mersey* at Liverpool. Phoned my wife in the Lake District and learned that the *Voltaire* had been sunk. This news was given by Lord Haw Haw. Needless to say my family were overjoyed as they had feared me lost, being ignorant that I had left *Voltaire*.

After a few weeks leave, during which time I received a letter from the Admiralty stating that since I had relinquished my commission in the RNR I was no longer entitled to wear the RNR uniform. I was sent to Baltimore with a crew for a leaselend ship which Lamport & Holt were taking over. Went by the *Britannic* which was taking about 300 Merchant Navy Officers and men to man leaselend ships. Disembarked at Halifax thence by train to Baltimore via New York. Joined the S.S. *Willimantic* which was under refit, and dated from the First war. Left Baltimore on May 14, 1941 for Cape Town, thence Abadan Basrah, over to Bombay and to Calcutta, then Rangoon. Left Rangoon without Pilot, or clearance, as the Japanese were about to take over, there being air raids every day. Back to Calcutta, having run out of water and stores. At Calcutta loaded for Bank Line for Beira and all ports – south to Cape Town. Left Cape Town, and after three days received orders to proceed to Charleston, USA.

Author's Note: Loss of this vessel appears later, as does that of the *Browning*.

Joined *Balfe* in January, 1943 as Chief Officer at London. Later joined a convoy for passage to New York. Broke the glass in my sextant in heavy weather, it being the only one on board. The 3rd Engineer had a ladies handbag mirror which I managed to cut with paraffin and string, and fitted it and after an hour got it adjusted. Weather hellish, in fact rigged a jury stay sail to help steering. Loaded general cargo at New York which included a few hundred tons of TNT in No. 2 hold, and several landing craft on deck. Sailed independent for Boston to join a large convoy. First night out from Boston about 0100 we were in collision with the Dutch ship *Boskoop* which was in an outward bound convoy. She either didn't see his own Commodore's signal or did not understand it. The result was he collided with us – the leading ship in No. 2 column. Our bow was stove in completely. The double bottom was leaking, but the holds were intact. Detached from the convoy under escort and proceeded to Halifax, Nova Scotia, where a new bow was fitted, and finally sailed home in convoy. Next voyage in *Balfe* was to the River Plate with generals homewards. Sailed independently to Freetown to bunker and join a convoy. Destination Glasgow. Extremely bad weather SSW of Ireland, sustained extensive damage including loss of a lifeboat. I became very ill, but continued doing my duties. Eventually arriving at Glasgow on December 26, 1943. I was rushed to Govan General Hospital and had an emergency operation for a gangrenous appendicitis, and spent four weeks in hospital.

I joined the Lamport & Holt managed Liberty ship *Samana* in March, 1944 for a voyage to Bombay, Karachi and back home. Then loaded sea transport for Naples, Alexandria and Port Said. Thereafter based on Alexandria stayed in Mediterranean supplying the army in Italy, Libya and Greece. Left the Mediterranean light ship for French East Africa and there loaded a cargo of mahogany for the UK. The next voyage was sea transport for the Persian Gulf, Basrah, Abadan. Took on four heavy duty pumps for Bombay to pump out the docks after the explosion. Discharged at Bombay, and then based on Singapore running military supplies to Java, Rangoon, the Philippines, Kure, Japan. War over, I even visited Hiroshima a few months after the Atom bomb had been dropped. A scene of complete devastation. Finally bordering on a nervous breakdown I was relieved in *Samana* at Singapore on medical advice and returned home on the troopship *Monarch of Bermuda* in September, 1946. The strain of the war years with no let up, very little leave, had at last caught up with me, but with a few weeks convalescence with my wife and family, I quickly recovered.

Lamport & Holt having acquired two Victory Ships, I was sent to join one the *Villar* at Portland, Oregon on November 19, 1946 as Chief Officer. Captain Kemmings in command. Loaded at San Francisco and Los Angeles, sailed via the Panama Canal, for London then Liverpool, arriving on March 15, 1947. Sailed on April 11 for the West Indies and the Amazon, then carried out a regular service between New York, Brazil and the River Plate, until July 20, 1948 I returned home via Cunard. After a months leave joined the *Delane* as Chief Officer on October 28,

1948 (Captain Pratt in command) remained in this vessel on the UK/South America service for eleven voyages until October 2, 1951.

While on leave I was appointed to command the *Delane* for her next voyage. In the meantime Captain Bibby *Sallust* New York service was taken ill in New York, and I was sent over passenger in the *Queen Elizabeth* to take over command from him. Joining her November 1951 remained on the South American service from New York until December, 1952 when I brought the vessel home to the UK. After leave, rejoined *Sallust* in March, 1953 and sailed from Antwerp to Montreal and continued on the New York, Brazil and River Plate service until relieved at Paranagua in February, 1954 and came home as passenger on the *Delius* for home leave. Spent the next four months coasting on *Lassell*, *Sallust* and *Delius*.

I was appointed Master of *Spenser* (later to become *Roscoe*) an ex-German ship at New York, whose master was hospitalised. I flew over from London and joined the ship after clearance at customs 5.8.1954 – 1350 hours. Sailed immediately for Brazil and the River Plate, then brought her home to the UK leaving in November, 1954. Thereafter I was master of *Balzac*, an ex-Norwegian reefer from January 10, 1955 carrying bananas from Santos for seven voyages until December of that year. I spent the next eighteen months as master of the *Roscoe* for six voyages from the UK, and after two weeks coasting on the *Lassell*, was appointed to the *Romney* on September 2, 1957 for three voyages from the UK to South America, and followed by six voyages on the Montreal, West Indies, Georgetown service, until arriving in the UK on March 18, 1959. I served on the *Rubens* for eight months from the UK, and thereafter spent a period coasting around the UK.

On April 20, 1960 I was appointed master of our newest UK based vessel *Ronsard* and carried out 33 voyages on the UK/South American service until May, 1970. I had been appointed commodore in 1967, and attended a Queens Garden Party in1969. After a short period relieving I retired in December 1970 after 46 years service.

When I joined the firm in 1924 I think the company was at its peak. There were around 54 vessels in the fleet. Regular services from the United Kingdom and New York to Brazil and the River Plate. Three vessels regularly carried emigrants from Spain and Portugal. While four 'V' class ships – 1st class passenger ships from New York and were every popular. The ships I recall were always loaded full and down to their marks, and I should imagine that Lamport & Holt ships carried the bulk of the coffee beans into the States. I recall counting ten Lamport & Holt ships in Santos on one occasion loading and discharging. On approaching Buenos Aires docks one could not miss seeing several black, white and blue funnels.

Of the Captains, Officers and the Men, they were loyal to the extreme, and I shall always be proud to have known and sailed with them.

FLEET LIST Part 7

| *Laplace* (2) 1919-1942 | 7,327 | Steamship. 1919 built by A. McMillan and Son Ltd., Dumbarton, for Liverpool, Brazil & River Plate Steam Navigation Co. Ltd. (Lamport & Holt Ltd.); 1934 to Lamport & Holt Line Ltd.; 29.10.1942 torpedoed and sunk by *U159* South East of Cape Agulhas. |

The *Laplace* (2) of 1919.
(*World Ship Photo Library*)

A wartime view of the *Laplace* with gun fitted aft.   *(A. Duncan)*

Name & Period in Fleet	Gross tons	History
Nasmyth (2) 1919-1938	6,509	Steamship. 1919 built by Harland & Wolff Ltd., Belfast, as *War Vision* for the Shipping Controller; 1919 to Liverpool, Brazil & River Plate Steam Navigation Co. Ltd. (Lamport & Holt Ltd.); renamed *Nasmyth*; 1934 to Lamport & Holt Line Ltd.; 11.1938 broken up by F. Rysdyk, Rotterdam, in damaged condition following stranding at Tanife Point, South Grand Canary Island on 1.5.1938.
Newton (3) 1919-1933	6,509	Steamship. 1919 built by Harland & Wolff Ltd., Belfast, as *War Justice* for the Shipping Controller; 1919 to Liverpool, Brazil & River Plate Steam Navigation Co. Ltd. (Lamport & Holt Ltd.); 1933 to Rethymnis and Kulukundis, Piraeus, renamed *Mount Othrys*; 6.1.1945 lost in collision in the River Thames, on passage from St. John, New Brunswick to London, declared a Constructive Total Loss, and broken up.
Biela (2) 1919-1942	5,298	Steamship. 1918 built by Short Bros. Ltd., Sunderland, as *War Mastiff* for the Shipping Controller; 1919 to Liverpool, Brazil & River Plate Steam Navigation Co. Ltd. (Lamport & Holt Ltd.); renamed *Biela*; 1934 to Lamport & Holt Line Ltd.; 14.2.1942 missing; transpired that had been torpedoed and sunk by *U98* East of Cape Race, while on passage Liverpool to Buenos Aires.

The *Biela* (2) was one of nine 'B' class vessels acquired from the Shipping Controller following the First World War.
(World Ship Photo Library)

On February 14, 1942 the *Biela* on passage Liverpool to Buenos Aires, unescorted and alone disappeared East of Cape Race, having sent a radio message stating she was being attacked – which was picked up by the ship *Start Point*. It later transpired that she was torpedoed and sunk by U98, with the loss of her entire crew of 56.

(World Ship Photo Library)

Name & Period in Fleet	Gross tons	History
Bernini 1919-1933	5,242	Steamship. 1918 built by W. Dobson and Co. Ltd., Newcastle, as *War Penguin* for Shipping Controller; 1919 to Liverpool, Brazil & River Plate Steam Navigation Co. Ltd. (Lamport & Holt Ltd.), renamed *Bernini*; 1933 to Rethymnis and Kulukundis, Piraeus, renamed *Mount Dirfys*; 26.12.1936 wrecked on Frying Pan Shoals, Norfolk, Virginia.
Delambre (2) 1919-1940	7,032	Steamship. 1917 built by Mitsubishi Zosen Kaisha, Nagasaki, as *War Dame* for the Shipping Controller; 1919 to Liverpool, Brazil & River Plate Steam Navigation Co. Ltd. (Lamport & Holt Ltd.); renamed *Delambre*; 1934 to Lamport & Holt Line Ltd.; 7.7.1940 sunk by the raider *Thor* North West of Ascension Island.

The World War 1 standard ship *Delambre* (2) was built in Japan in 1917 and acquired in 1919.

(World Ship Photo Library)

Name & Period in Fleet	Gross tons	History
Bronte 1919-1939	5,314	Steamship. 1919 built by A. McMillan and Son Ltd., Dumbarton, as *War Coney* for the Shipping controller; 1919 to Liverpool, Brazil & River Plate Steam Navigation Co. Ltd. (Lamport & Holt Ltd.), renamed *Bronte*; 1934 to Lamport & Holt Line Ltd.; 27.10.1939 torpedoed by *U34* South West of Ireland; 30.10.1939 sunk by escorts HMS *Warpole* and HMS *Whirlwind* after having tried to tow her in.

The *Bronte* (1).
  (World Ship Photo Library)

Browning (1) 1919-1942	5,332	Steamship. 1919 built by A. McMillan and Son Ltd., Dumbarton, as *War Marten* for the Shipping Controller; 1919 to Liverpool, Brazil & River Plate Steam Navigation Co. Ltd. (Lamport & Holt Ltd.), renamed *Browning*; 1934 to Lamport & Holt Line Ltd.; 12.11.1942 torpedoed and sunk by *U595* off Oran.

The *Browning* (1).
  (A. Duncan)

Name & Period in Fleet	Gross tons	History
Bruyere 1919-1942	5,335	Steamship. 1919 built by A. McMillan and Son Ltd., Dumbarton, as *War Mole* for the Shipping Controller; 1919 to Liverpool, Brazil & River Plate Steam Navigation Co. Ltd. (Lamport & Holt Ltd.), renamed *Bruyere*; 1934 to Lamport & Holt Line Ltd.; 23.9.1942 torpedoed and sunk by *U125* South West of Freetown, while on passage Buenos Aires to the United Kingdom.
Balfe 1919-1950	5,369	Steamship. 1919 built by D. & W. Henderson and Co. Ltd., Glasgow as *War Lupin* for the Shipping Controller; 1919 to Liverpool, Brazil & River Plate Steam Navigation Co. Ltd. (Lamport & Holt Ltd.), renamed *Balfe*; 1934 to Lamport & Holt Line Ltd.; 1950 to Ali A. Hoborby (Jas. Norris and Company), Liverpool, renamed *Star of Aden*; 1955 to John Manners and Co. Ltd., Hong Kong, renamed *Sydney Breeze*; 1955 to World Wide Steamship Co. Ltd., Hong Kong, renamed *Golden Beta*; 1.2.1959 arrived at Osaka for breaking up by Mitsubishi Zosen Kaisha.

The *Balfe* at Buenos Aires.
(*National Maritime Museum*)

Another view of the *Balfe*. (*A. Duncan*)

Name & Period in Fleet	Gross tons	History
Bonheur 1920-1940	5,327	Steamship. 1920 built by Harland & Wolff Ltd., Belfast, for the Shipping Controller; 1920 completed as *Bonheur* for Liverpool, Brazil & River Plate Steam Navigation Co. Ltd. (Lamport & Holt Ltd.); 1934 to Lamport & Holt Line Ltd.; 15.10.1940 torpedoed and sunk by *U138* North West of Cape Wrath, while on passage from Liverpool to Rosario.

The *Bonheur* of 1920.
(National Maritime Museum)

The *Bonheur*. *(A. Duncan)*

Name & Period in Fleet	Gross tons	History

Balzac (1)
1920-1941

5,372

Steamship. 1920 built by D. & W. Henderson and Co. Ltd., Glasgow as *War Yew* for the Shipping Controller; 1920 completed as *Balzac* for Liverpool, Brazil & River Plate Steam Navigation Co. Ltd. (Lamport & Holt Ltd.); 1934 to Lamport & Holt Line Ltd.; 22.6.1941 sunk by the raider *Atlantis* North East of Para, on a voyage Rangoon to Liverpool.

The *Balzac* (1).
(A. Duncan)

Boswell (1)
1920-1933

5,327

Steamship. 1920 built by Harland & Wolff Ltd., Belfast, for the Shipping Controller; 1920 completed as *Boswell* for Liverpool, Brazil & River Plate Steam Navigation Co. Ltd. (Lamport & Holt Ltd.); 1933 to White Steamship Co. Ltd., renamed *Adderstone*; 1937 to J. Gerrard, Kristiansand, renamed *Gema*; 1950 to Wallem and Company, Hong Kong (Panamanian flag); 1951 to Daichi K.K., Kobe, renamed *Norway Maru*; 1958 re-engined as a motorship; 1968 broken up at Sakai.

The *Boswell* (1).
(A. Duncan)

Name & Period in Fleet	Gross tons	History
Lalande (2) 1920-1950	7,453	Steamship. 1920 built by D. & W. Henderson Co. Ltd., Glasgow for Liverpool, Brazil & River Plate Steam Navigation Co. Ltd. (Lamport & Holt Ltd.); 1934 to Lamport & Holt Line Ltd.; 1950 to Gestioni Esercizio Navi-GEN, Genoa, renamed *Cristina Maria G*; 1953 to Rasmar Inc., Panama, renamed *Cristina Maria*; 8.8.1959 arrived at Hamburg for breaking up by W. Ritscher.

The *Lalande* (2).
(World Ship Photo Library)

Leighton 1921-1946	7,412	Motorship. 1921 built by A. McMillan and Son Ltd., Dumbarton, for Liverpool, Brazil & River Plate Steam Navigation Co. Ltd. (Lamport & Holt Ltd.); 1934 to Lamport & Holt Line Ltd.; 28.8.1946 to Smith and Houston Ltd., Port Glasgow, for breaking up, but laid up in the Gareloch; 1947 to Ministry of Defence; 9.8.1947 scuttled in North Atlantic, 100 miles North West of Malin Head, with a cargo of wartime gas bombs.

The twin-screw motorship *Leighton* arrived in 1921.
(World Ship Photo Library)

Name & Period in Fleet	Gross tons	History
Linnell 1921-1939	7,424	Motorship. 1921 built by A. McMillan and Son Ltd., Dumbarton, for Liverpool, Brazil & River Plate Steam Navigation Co. Ltd. (Lamport & Holt Ltd.); 1934 to Lamport & Holt Line Ltd.; 1939 stranded at Alexandria, refloated, but badly damaged; 23.8.1939 arrived at Troon for breaking up.

The motorship *Linnell*.
(A. Duncan)

Name & Period in Fleet	Gross tons	History
Hogarth (2) 1921-1933	8,109	Steamship. 1921 built by D. & W. Henderson and Co. Ltd., Glasgow, for Liverpool, Brazil & River Plate Steam Navigation Co. Ltd. (Lamport & Holt Ltd); 17.8.1933 arrived at Port Glasgow for breaking up by Smith and Houston Ltd.
Vandyck (3) 1921-1940	13,233	Steamship. 1921 built by Workman, Clark and Co. Ltd., Belfast, for Liverpool, Brazil & River Plate Steam Navigation Co. Ltd. (Lamport & Holt Ltd.); 1934 to Lamport & Holt Ltd.; 10.1939 converted to an armed boarding vessel – HMS *Vandyck*; 10.6.1940 bombed and sunk West of Narvik.
Lassell (2) 1922-1941	7,417	Motorship. 1922 built by A. McMillan and Son Ltd., Dumbarton, for Liverpool, Brazil & River Plate Steam Navigation Co. Ltd. (Lamport & Holt Ltd.); 1934 to Lamport & Holt Line Ltd.; 30.4.1941 torpedoed and sunk by *U107* South West of Cape Verde Islands.
Voltaire (2) 1923-1941	13,248	Steamship. 1923 built by Workman, Clark and Co. Ltd., Belfast, for Liverpool, Brazil & River Plate Steam Navigation Co. Ltd. (Lamport & Holt Ltd.); 1934 to Lamport & Holt Line Ltd.; 10.1939 converted to armed merchant cruiser – HMS *Voltaire*; 9.4.1941 sunk by the raider *Thor*.

The liner *Voltaire* (2) at sea. (A. Duncan)

The *Voltaire* dressed overall at anchor.   *(World Ship Photo Library)*

Name & Period in Fleet	Gross tons	History
Delius 1937-1954 1958-1961	6,065	Motorship. 1937 built by Harland & Wolff Ltd., Belfast, for Lamport & Holt Line Ltd.; 1941 re-measured, tonnage increased to 7,783 gross; 1954 to Blue Star Line Ltd., renamed *Portland Star*; 1958 bareboat chartered to Lamport & Holt Line Ltd., renamed *Delius*; 1961 to Cie. Metallurgique et Miniere, Casablanca, renamed *Kettara VII*; 24.2.1962 arrived at Tokyo for breaking up by Izumi-Ohtsu.

The *Delius* – a revolution in cargo liner design in the 1930s.

(A. Duncan)

Name & Period in Fleet	Gross tons	History
Delane 1938-1954	6,054	Motorship. 1938 built by Harland & Wolff Ltd., Belfast, for Lamport & Holt Line Ltd.; 1941 re-measured, tonnage increased to 7,761 gross; 1954 to Blue Star Line Ltd., renamed *Seattle Star*; 1961 to Cie Metallurgique et Miniere, Casablanca, renamed *Kettara VI*; 13.10.1961 arrived at Hong Kong for breaking up by Hong Kong Rolling Mills Ltd.

The *Delane*.
(A. Duncan)

Name & Period in Fleet	Gross tons	History
Devis (1) 1938-1943	6,054	Motorship. 1938 built by Harland & Wolff Ltd., Belfast, for Lamport & Holt Line Ltd.; 1941 re-measured, tonnage increased to 7,761 gross; 5.7.1943 torpedoed and sunk by *U693* off the coast of Sicily.

The defensively armed merchant ship *Devis* (1).
(A. Duncan)

9. THE SECOND WORLD WAR

At the outbreak of the Second World War the fleet consisted of twenty-one ships of which fourteen were to be lost during the period of hostilities, including the two last passenger liners, *Vandyck* and *Voltaire*, whilst on service with the Royal Navy.

Owing to the threat of hostilities all cruising ceased and the *Voltaire* and *Vandyck* were quickly converted for the carriage of troops. In June, 1939 the *Voltaire* sailed for Bombay with troops carrying homewards a number of NCO's and their families. While passing through the Bay of Biscay an Admiralty 'A' message was received warning that hostilities were imminent. Arriving at Southampton on August 28, she disembarked her passengers, and, the crew not being allowed ashore, the ship was painted grey overall and the following evening sailed for Scapa Flow.

At Scapa the *Voltaire* served as a hostel ship for the services, and was anchored close to H.M.S. *Iron Duke*. She was there when war was declared and when H.M.S. *Royal Oak* was sunk, and on the morning after this last event was present when German aircraft made an attack on H.M.S. *Iron Duke*. Although one of the aircraft was shot down a hit was scored on the *Iron Duke* which necessitated her having to be beached. The *Voltaire* at this time had all the survivors from the *Royal Oak* on board, and the master, expecting another attack, wisely put these ashore at Flotta Island until nightfall. Hardly had this been carried out, when another air attack commenced, the *Voltaire* being the target on this occasion, and although a number of near misses were registered, and a small amount of damage was caused to the ship, she survived the experience. The following day the *Voltaire* was renamed *Iron Duke II*, replacing the original.

At the end of October 1939 the *Iron Duke II (Voltaire)* sailed from Scapa Flow for Newcastle. There at the yard of Swan Hunter and Wigham Richardson Ltd. she was refitted and converted into an armed merchant cruiser. Her main armament comprised eight-6 inch breech loading guns, which came from the old H.M.S. *Tiger* of Jutland fame. Most of the peacetime officers, at the request of Lamport & Holt, stayed with the ship, which had now become H.M.S. *Voltaire*.

In January 1940 she sailed for Malta, where she was on contraband control, with an area of patrol from the Adriatic Eastwards to the Dardanelles. After being employed on such duties, she left the Mediterranean in June 1940, and was then employed escorting convoys across the North Atlantic, mainly from Halifax, but on occasions from Bermuda. It was while so employed that the *Voltaire* was lost. She had left Halifax, Nova Scotia, had called at Trinidad, and was en route to Freetown for a convoy, when in the early morning of April 9, 1941 she fell in with the German armed raider *Thor*, and after a heavy battle, was sunk by the superior gunfire of the German vessel. A total of 197 survivors were picked up by the raider, all of which were to spend the remainder of the war as prisoners in Germany.

Shortly after the outbreak

In 1989 a diver at Scapa Flow discovered two plates lying on the sea bed. Clearly they had gone overboard from the *Voltaire* in 1939. *(P.M. Heaton)*

of war the *Vandyck* was taken over by the Admiralty, and was converted to an armed boarding vessel — H.M.S. *Vandyck*. She was to survive until June 10, 1940, when en route to take part in the evacuation of troops from Norway, she was bombed and sunk by an enemy aircraft off the Norwegian coast, while under the command of Captain G.F.W. Wilson, RN. Two officers and five ratings were lost; 29 officers and 132 ratings having landed, were taken prisoner by the Germans and were to be incarcerated in Germany for the remainder of the war.

Having dealt with the loss of the two passenger ships on service with the Royal Navy, we come to the losses suffered by the ships left on service with the company. The first casualty suffered by Lamport and Holt was the *Bronte* which was torpedoed by the German submarine *U34* in home waters on October 27, 1939, outward bound for South America, with a crew of forty and one passenger, a 71 year old inventor, fortunately without loss of life. The *Bronte* remained afloat for some time, and having at first been abandoned, some of the crew were put back on board in an attempt to tow the ship into port. However, these efforts were thwarted by the bad weather, and eventually three days later she was sunk by a charge set by her escort. Captain S. Dickinson, who was to become the cargo superintendent at Liverpool, was serving as third officer in the *Bronte* at the time.

On April 27, 1940 the *Delius* was damaged by an air attack whilst lying at Romsdalsfjord, Norway, a direct hit being recorded. This attack was to last two days.

On July 7, of the same year, the *Delambre* was proceeding homeward from South America to join a convoy at Freetown, when she was intercepted by the German raider *Thor*, which was later to account for the loss of the *Voltaire*. After a two hour chase by the raider, the much slower *Delambre* was overhauled and forced to stop. (Captain Pratt of the *Delambre* was captured in similar fashion by the raider *Moewe* in the earlier war). After transferring the crew to the raider, the *Delambre* was sunk. The crew were to remain in the raider for some time, before being transferred to an auxiliary, which was to land them in occupied territory. The late Hugh Binney, well remembered at Lamport and Holt, was serving as ship's carpenter at the time, and he related how he left his home on May 6, 1940, not arriving back until exactly five years to the day, having spent most of the intervening period as a prisoner of war in Germany.

On October 15, 1940 the *Bonheur* was torpedoed and sunk by the submarine *U138* while outward bound in convoy, Liverpool to Rosario, the sinking taking place in home waters. The following month, on November 19, the *Biela* was damaged by an aircraft attack in position 52.26'N, 16.31'W; and on the night of December 20/21, the *Laplace* was damaged by a bomb while lying at Liverpool. On February 26, 1941 the *Swinburne* was bombed and sunk by German aircraft in home waters. On April 6, the same year the *Devis* was damaged by an air attack while lying at Piraeus.

During 1940 two further 'D' class ships were added to the fleet, the *Debrett* and *Defoe*, both coming, like their earlier sisters, from Harland and Wolff Ltd., Belfast. There were now five of this class trading for the company.

The next loss was the *Lassell* which, having left Liverpool for South America under the command of Captain A.R. Bibby early in April 1941, was torpedoed on the evening of April 30, about 300 miles South West of the Cape Verde Islands. I quote hereunder the report made by the chief officer to the owners on his return to the United Kingdom, in full, as it is an interesting account of the loss and subsequent journey in one of the lifeboats.

M.V. Lassell

Account of the loss through enemy action, and log of the survivors in No. 3 Boat.
H.W. Underhill – Chief Officer
D. Enticknap – 3rd Officer

Wednesday, April 30, 1941
Noon – In position latitude 13.55' North, longitude 28.59' West True course S 7 E. Speed 10.2 knots. Moderate NE breeze. Slight sea and moderate NE swell. Cloudy, fine and clear.

18.02 – In position latitude 12.55' North, longitude 28.50' West. The vessel was struck by a torpedo on the port side in the engine room near No. 4 bulkhead. No. 4 boat was smashed and thrown inboard. All W/T gear rendered useless. Both engines stopped instantly and the engine room flooded. The vessel listed about 10 degrees to port and returned to an even keel almost immediately. She then commenced to settle by the stern, and the abandon ship signal was given. No. 2 boat was lowered, but, owing to the vessel's way and the effect of the swell, was damaged against the ship's side and had to be abandoned. Nos. 1 and 3 boats were lowered and manned, although the work was rendered difficult by quantities of fuel oil and sheep dip which were forced by the air pressure out of the engine room and No. 4 hold ventilators onto the boat deck.

18.03 – No. 3 boat with the 3rd officer in charge, cleared the ship with twenty men.

18.09 – No. 1 boat with Captain Bibby in charge, cleared the ship with chief and 2nd officers, twenty-six men and one lady passenger.

18.10 – The vessel foundered stern first at an angle of approximately 60 deg. The mainmast crumpled and fell to the deck as she went under. A quantity of flotsam, including a number of rafts, and a pedigree bull floated clear.

18.15 – A very large submarine marked *U22* (although it has been confirmed that it was *U107* which was responsible for the loss of the vessel) surfaced about three hundred yards from the boats and opened fire with machine guns on the bull which was struggling in the water. Both boats lay to.

18.20 – The submarine dived. No. 3 boat pulled to the wreckage of No. 2 boat and salvaged one case corned beef, two cases condensed milk and two casks water.

18.45 – Night fell, both boats laying to sea anchors and maintained communication by flashing torches.

Thursday, May 1

At 05.00 No. 3 boat pulled to No. 1 boat half-a-mile distant. Chief Officer Underhill and four men were transferred from No. 1 boat. It was then definitely established that only two men missing were 3rd Engineer J. Chaney and Greaser W. Quinn. As both these men were in the engine room at the time of the torpedo struck the ship they were assumed to have been trapped by the inrush of water and drowned.

Both boats lay to sea anchors throughout the day and No. 1 boat used the portable radio transmitter at two-hourly intervals.

At 16.00 a large unidentified steamer was sighted about four miles off to the eastward. The radio transmitter was used, and No. 3 boat burned two red flares. The vessel maintained her course to the northward and passed from sight. The first ration of water and biscuits was issued in No. 3 boat at 18.00.

Both boats lay to sea anchors as on the previous night.

Friday, May 2

No. 3 boat pulled over to No. 1 boat at daylight and reported to Captain Bibby for orders. One 7 gallon cask of fresh water was transferred to No. 1 boat. Both boats lay to until 08.00 when sails were hoisted and course set to NE x E true (E x E magnetic) in an endeavour to reach the Cape Verde Islands. This was found to be impossible, and No. 3 boat, sailing as close to the wind as she could, made SE x E true.

No. 1 boat seemed to be sailing a little closer to the wind, but both boats made a great deal of leeway.

At 11.00 the top gudgeon on the stern post of No. 3 boat carried away, rendering the rudder useless. This was therefore jettisoned and the sweep oar rigged as a jury rudder and served fairly satisfactorily.

At 16.00 No. 3 boat, when about three miles ahead of No. 1 hove to, to enable her to close before nightfall. No. 1 boat maintained her course and passed to windward. No. 3 reset her sails and proceeded.

Communication was established, but at 23.00 No. 3 boat failed to receive any answer to her signals, and although the torch was used at frequent intervals the two boats never regained touch.

Saturday, May 3

From here on this account is written as the Log Book of No. 3 boat alone.

As we were now alone we decided to take stock of our resources and come to some definite organisation and routine.

The following is a list of the boat's personnel:

Name	*Rank*
H.W. Underhill	Chief Officer
D. Enticknap	3rd officer
A.B. Withers	6th engineer
J. Simpson	7th engineer
H. Hutton	3rd radio officer
P.J. Guy	Cadet
K. Elgin	Cadet
G. Robinson	AB
J. Blundell	AB
J. Graham	AB

J. Quinn	AB
D. Leicester	OS
W. Parry	OS
H. Scott	Deck boy
J. Sullivan	Greaser
T. Wake	2nd steward
E. McArdle	Assistant steward
A. Buck	Steward's boy
W. Childs	Private, R.M.
J. Allingham	Seaman Gunner
F.H. Butler	Bombardier, R.A.
W. Wilkinson	Gunner, R.A.
P. Giffard	Gunner, R.A.
H. Bolch	Gunner, R.A.
J. Holmes	Gunner, R.A.
T. Caddy	Gunner, R.A.

The crew were divided into three sections. Six men living in the bow of the boat were made responsible for the lookout at night. The seventeen men amidships kept the day lookout and bailed whenever necessary (usually twice a day). The chief and 3rd officers and A.B. Robinson kept two-hour watches at the steering oar. 6th engineer Withers, having been badly burned on the left arm and side by blazing fuel oil in the engine room, was exempted from all duties.

The stores were checked over, and the following list drawn up. This includes the boat's own stores and those salvaged from No. 2 boat:

24 gallons fresh water in one 10 gallon and two 7 gallon casks.

112 lbs biscuits in two airtight containers.

72 lbs Nestles sweetened condensed milk in 1 lb tins.

120 lbs Armour's corned beef in forty-eight 1 kilo tins.

500 Gold Flake cigarettes in ten tins of 50.

20 lifeboat matches in watertight container.

One First Aid outfit.

12 blankets.

24 Regulation red flares (two of these were used yesterday).

Apart from this list there was the usual lifeboat equipment specified by the Ministry of Shipping and a number of cigarettes and matches in the private possession of various members of the crew. This seemed a fairly satisfactory list of provisions, and the only question which gave rise to any anxiety was that of matches. It was decided not to pool them, but orders were issued for the strictest economy, and when cigarettes were issued after the morning and evening meals, one match only was used to light the entire 21. (There were only five non-smokers).

The menu decided on was as follows:

07.00 – One biscuit covered with corned beef, followed by a cigarette.

Noon – Two spoonfuls of condensed milk and one full dipper of water (quarter-pint).

17.30 – The same as at 07.00 but with the addition of a half a dipper of water.

This proved to be an extremely economical bill of fare as it exactly used a 1 kilo tin of meat each meal. At midday too, the ration of milk emptied a 1lb tin. The tin was then passed to one of the younger, and more junior members of the crew, to be cleaned out, usually by licking the forefinger, after which its edges were bent down and it served as a drinking mug.

Sunday, May 4

Course maintained. Estimated speed 2 to 3 knots. It was realised that it would be impossible to make the Cape Verdes as the wind was steadily NE to ENE and Force 2 to 4. The main objective was to make as much easting as possible, in order to get into the convoy tracks near Freetown, and ultimately to reach the African coast, about 900 miles distant, should we not be picked up. As there were no instruments of any sort except the compass, any attempt at navigation, beyond guesswork, was impossible. Nevertheless, it was realised that should we go too far North, which was unlikely, we should land in enemy territory and be interned. On the other hand, should we go too far Southward, which seemed to be the tendency, we should eventually sail into the Gulf of Guinea, which would more than double the distance required to make a landfall. However this was all conjecture, and there was very little question in anyone's mind that a convoy would soon be sighted.

This being a Sunday, a double ration of water was issued at noon, and it was decided that for the next few days the water ration could be increased to two dippers (half pint) per man per day, by the issue of a half dipper at the morning meal.

Monday, May 5

Maintained course. Usual daily routine. The general attitude of the men seemed optimistic and fairly certain that we should be picked up at any time. The wind dropped almost completely at sunset but anti-Trade winds were seen about 21.00. The lower clouds, cumulus stratus, were moving in a SW direction, and the higher banks, consisting principally of cirrus clouds, in a NE'ly. These were rain clouds to the westward, but a change of wind to the SW seemed to be indicated which, it was hoped, would bring them nearer. In view of this possibility a plan for trapping as much rainwater as possible was drawn up, so that no time should be wasted if the rains came.

The men turned in in the usual manner, laying athwart the boat on the oars, which were spread out evenly in the centre. Those who had overcoats wore them, and with a few exceptions there was one blanket to each two men. The boat cover was also spread as an added protection against the damp atmosphere at night and the early morning dew.

Tuesday, May 6

At about 08.00 the wind veered to SE x S, so course was altered to E x N (magnetic), allowing two points Westerly error and three points for leeway, to make NNE true. It was a comparatively uneventful day but a deal hotter than those previous. Night fell with a promise of rain. The chief officer obtained an error of the compass by bringing the Pole Star right ahead. This gave an error of almost three points West. The variation was believed to be about 20 deg. West, so the resulting deviation of 14 deg. was assumed to be caused by the proximity of the compass to the after lifting hook of the boat. However the compass was steady and behaving admirably so things were left as they were.

Wednesday, May 7

All hands on deck at 04.00 to catch rain. The sail was lowered and prepared as had previously been arranged but after a few drops the shower passed overhead so the sail was reset and the boat got under way again.

The wind this morning was light and variable, and several men felt that it would be more satisfactory to be pulling on the oars than laying almost becalmed. The mainsail was lowered and the oars manned, but after half an hour it was found to be too wearying in proportion to the progress made, and the attempt was abandoned.

At 11.00 a bathing parade was organised. Each man was permitted to go over the side for a few minutes, but strict orders were issued not to leave hold of the becket lines. While this was in progress an extra man was posted to keep a lookout for sharks. The effect of this dip was excellent; apart from cooling the body and tending to allay thirst it was very heartening to feel that the boat was actually making way, however little, through the water.

It was a week today that the ship was lost. Everybody was still fairly cheerful about things, and usually somebody would say at daylight, "Thank goodness we are going to be picked up today". There was no despondency and mild wagers were being laid as to the exact day and time when the rescue ship would come along. A prize of ten shillings was offered for the first person to sight a ship, and should she subsequently stop and take us aboard it was to be increased to thirty shillings. The rescue ship was never referred to as such, but as 'Our Good Neighbour Ship". This was because a certain American company uses this as their slogan, and an American steamer had been heard transmitting a weather bulletin the day before the ship was lost.

The average temperatures were estimated today to be about 98 deg. Fahrenheit by day, and 65 by night.

Thursday, May 8

At daybreak the wind backed to the NE again so the SE'ly course was resumed. The weather continued as before, slight sea and low easterly swell.

At the morning meal today the first cask of water was emptied. This meant that 26 men had consumed seven gallons in seven days. There still remained one seven and one ten gallon casks, so at the present, rather liberal rate of consumption, this would have been sufficient for a further seventeen days. Any rain caught would considerably lengthen that period. The question of food had, so far, provoked no anxiety. The meat was being consumed at the rate of two tins a day, but there still remained 36. Biscuits had recently fallen into disfavour as they seemed to be thirst provoking. Some men had been finding the meat indigestible during the last two days, and had been having the alternative of two spoonfuls of milk. To date, only eight of the 72 tins of milk had been used.

At about 21.00 a small squid climbed aboard the boat. It had a flying fish firmly grasped in its tentacles. It was slightly larger than a clenched fist, with a dull red colouring and two small, beady eyes protruding from its head. It was hastily ejected and dropped back into the water.

Friday, May 9

Wind NE. Force 4. Moderate sea and swell. The boat seemed to be making about three and a half knots and was spraying forward occasionally. In order to get as much speed as possible the bathing parade was cancelled today.

There were a number of cases requiring medical treatment. 6th Engineer Withers' arm was washed and redressed. It was still raw, but quite clean and seemed to be progressing as well as might be expected under the circumstances.

Gunner Holmes complained of a cut in his thumb which was badly swollen. This was the first time this man had reported sick although he suffered this cut in abandoning the ship over a week ago. He said that it had become much worse overnight and, on questioning, admitted that he had been one of the men who had handled that squid yesterday evening. The wound was cleansed and dressed, but it obviously needed better treatment than anyone in the boat was in a position to give it.

In the afternoon there were two more patients. One man complained of feeling faint. Aged 21, he was very slight, and seemed less able to stand the strain than the others. He was given sal volatile, and for the rest of the afternoon, and all night, he dozed fitfully, sometimes striking out at those next to him and all the time moaning quietly or mumbling incoherencies to himself.

The other was simply a case of sunstoke and despondency. He was the first man to, in any way, intimate that he was on the verge of giving up hope of being rescued. In this case sal volatile had less effect that a few well-chosen words, but after the heat of the day had passed he seemed to have less difficulty with his breathing, and eventually slept with a certain amount of ease.

After the evening meal the boat was bailed, and before turning in at 19.00 A.B. Blundell and 2nd Steward Wake requested that they might hold a small prayer service for the benefit of any Roman Catholics that were present. It was thought that it would be invidious to make any distinction as to creed and it was decided that anyone who wished to might join in. This met with unanimous response and Wake led the boat's company in the Lord's Prayer, followed, after a few moments of silent meditation, by an impromptu plea for a speedy rescue, both for us and for the crew of the No. 1 boat, of which we had seen nothing for eight days. All hands then piped down except the officer of the watch and the lookout man.

Saturday, May 10

At 05.15 everyone was awakened as the chief officer sang out: "Men, a ship. God has answered our prayer".

In the breaking dawn a small dot was seen on the horizon to Westward and a matter of seconds later a red flare had been ignited and was being waved aloft. It seemed at first that she was heading away and three more flares were burned in quick succession. She was then seen to alter course and steer straight for the boat. The sail was kept up for a few minutes longer for the sake of conspicuousness and a treble ration of water was issued to each man.

The sail was then lowered and neatly stowed, the oars were manned and the men were detailed to attend the boat hook and fenders. The ship approached, and was identified as the Elder Dempster liner *Egba*. She hove to to windward, and the boat was pulled over to her as she lowered guess warps and ladders. The men were in fine trim, and pulled on the oars with surprising strength. Once alongside, the boat was evacuated in an orderly manner. It was remarkable that with the exception of the 6th engineer, everyone was able to climb the pilot ladders without assistance. When aboard, the general physical weakness soon became apparent, and it was found almost impossible to remain standing, as the decks of the ship seemed to be lurching in every direction in a particularly violent fashion. Actually, she was lying in a flat calm with practically no movement at all, and our legs, which had been automatically counteracting the short, sharp motion of the boat for nine and a half days, were now creating a movement which did not really exist.

Egba hoisted the boat aboard her after deck and got under way. Mr. Underhill reported to the master, Captain G.D. Simpson, OBE., and supplied him with information necessary for his log book.

CONCLUSION

The position in which the boat was picked up by the *Egba* was latitude 10.57' North, longitude 29.13' West. Thus, our course and distance made good was S x W 120 miles. Our rough estimate had been SE 500 miles. This westerly set can only be explained as being due to the North East Trade Drift.

On being torpedoed we were 960 miles from Freetown, and 250 miles from Brava, the nearest of the Cape Verdes. Owing to the drift we had not diminished either of these distances, and that we were picked up at all, in that position, was plainly an act of Providence.

At 15.00 the same day, in position, latitude 11.11' North, longitude 27.53' West, the *Egba* sighted a second lifeboat. She closed it, and it was recognised as *Lassell's* No. 1 boat. It was empty, but bore signs of having recently been occupied. The mast had been unstepped and was lying on the thwarts. Several blankets hung over the side, apparently having been used as fenders. the portable radio transmitter was not in the boat, and there was very little water in the bottom. Everything seemed to indicate that her crew had been picked up not many hours previously.

The *Egba* did not pick it up, but continued her voyage to Freetown, where she arrived on the morning of Thursday, May 15.

During these five days, her officers and men did everything in their power to make us comfortable, frequently putting themselves to considerable inconvenience. Mr. Morris, the chief steward, was tireless in his capacity of doctor, dressing and attending the 6th engineer's arm and Gunner Holmes' hand at frequent intervals. It was his opinion that another two days without proper treatment would have seen the onset of serious complications in both cases.

No praise can be too high for the *Egba* ship's company and the entire boat's crew would like to have their very sincere gratitude recorded here.

On arrival at Freetown, a naval launch was sent out, and the chief officer, 6th engineer and 3rd radio officer were taken ashore to the flagship to make a report, while the 3rd officer, with Mr. Swannel of Elder Dempster Lines Ltd., arranged for the men to be accommodated at various hotels.

The eight DEMS ratings came under naval and military control and left the party.

It was arranged that an advance on wages should be issued to enable the men to purchase clothes and toilet necessities, as the naval authorities found themselves unable to do anything in this respect. The difficulty encountered here was that, apart from tropical kit, no clothes were obtainable in Freetown.

During our stay here, Mr. Wheeler, Elder Dempster's general manager, and Mr. Swannel did a great deal of organising on our behalf and secured the best accommodation available. Other ship survivors, who had different agencies, were considerably less well off than ourselves.

Two of the men, A.B. Quinn and O.S. Leicester, agreed to join a British merchant ship, the *Dahomian*, as AB's and commenced duty the following morning. This further reduction brought our party to sixteen, and that afternoon, Friday, May 16, we reported to the naval authorities and were conveyed to the New Zealand Shipping Company's liner *Ruahane* which sailed in convoy the next day, with a passenger list including 81 shipwrecked officers and men.

In conclusion, it seems appropriate to add, that the lifeboat, which was a standard 26-footer, built in 1921, was in every respect highly satisfactory, and made surprisingly little water. With the exception of the top gudgeon, which was pulled off the stern post, there was no untoward incident at all. The equipment was in good condition, especially the compass, which remained steady and easy to steer by throughout the voyage.

There were ample provisions. On being picked up there remained about 14 gallons of water, and milk and meat sufficient for a further seventeen days. The nutritive value of the milk cannot be overstressed. The meat, which for the first few days afforded a satisfying meal, had later tended to become indigestible.

The first aid equipment was satisfactory, aspirin and sal volatile being particularly useful.
(Signed)

      H.W. Underhill, Chief Officer
      D. Enticknap, 3rd Officer
      May 27, 1941
      Aboard *Ruahane*.

The occupants of No. 1 boat were rescued by the Ben Line steamer *Benvrackie* after nine days at sea, but were to face further hardships, for after four days the *Benvrackie* herself was torpedoed and sunk by the submarine *U105*. Fifteen of the original twenty-five who had been taken aboard the *Benvrackie* were lost at this time. The remaining ten, who included Captain Bibby, together with survivors from the Ben liner's crew, were to remain in an open boat for a further thirteen days, during which time a number of men died (none being from the *Lassell's* crew), before being picked up by a hospital ship and landed at Sierra Leone. It says much for their courage that they should survive this second ordeal.

Mr. Underhill after a period at home on leave was promoted master for his next voyage, taking over command of the steamer *Sheridan*. It will be noted that an ordinary seaman, who was amongst the occupants of the No. 3 lifeboat was called D. Leicester, and it is of interest that Mr. Underhill, while serving as second officer of the *Romney* in 1923 served under the command of his father. O.S. Leicester served with Lamport and Holt for many years, and himself rose to the rank of Captain with the company.

Incidentally, Captain Bibby had a brother-in-law who was also a master with the company, Captain W. Watson, and they each had a brother who served as chief officer with Lamport and Holt.

The *Phidias* was the next loss, under the command of Captain E. Parks. She was intercepted by the German submarine *U46* in the North Atlantic on June 8, 1941, which opened fire on the surface, and after a chase she discharged a torpedo which sank the *Phidias*, with the loss of eight of her crew of fifty-one.

The *Balzac* was the next of the fleet to be lost to the enemy, on June 22, 1941, and the following extract is taken from *The Secret Raiders* by David Woodward. (William Kimber, 1955)

On June 22, 1941, a ship was sighted from the German raider *Atlantis* at dawn. As the light improved she was seen to be a medium-sized armed vessel, towards which the *Atlantis* steered a collision course. Rogge (master of the *Atlantis*) opened fire at about 9,000 yards, and the enemy made RRR with her radio, which the *Atlantis* successfully jammed.

Then the British ship began zig-zagging and, handled very skillfully, presented the smallest possible target to her enemy. After forty salvoes – 190 rounds – had been fired by the Germans, only four hits had been made, and the forward 5.9 in. battery as well as the No. 5 gun broke down, owing to a defect in the recoil mechanisms. The guns were cooled with sea water and partly manhandled into position. While Rogge turned to bring the disengaged battery, on the other side of his ship, into action. As this was being done the enemy stopped and lowered her boats. She was the *Balzac* of 5,372 tons, from Rangoon to Liverpool with 4,200 tons of rice. Of her crew of forty-seven, four were killed.

In the long running fight the *Balzac* had had plenty of time to have got her RRR through and it was accordingly necessary for the *Atlantis* to disappear from the West side of the South Atlantic.

The *Balzac* was sunk, and the forty-three survivors were taken prisoner, and eventually arrived in Germany where they were to remain for the rest of the war. It had been a gallant effort by the *Balzac* to escape from the raider, but owing to her slow speed it was impossible, but she had still forced the raider to use valuable ammunition, and caused her to change her area of patrol.

The *Biela* under the command of Captain D. Anderson, left Liverpool on January 31, 1942, for Buenos Aires. On February 14, the steamer *Start Point* picked up a distress call indicating that the *Biela* was being attacked by a submarine about 400 miles South West of Cape Race. Nothing was ever heard of the *Biela* or her crew of forty-nine, and it was assumed that she had succumbed to a submarine attack. After the war it was confirmed by German sources that she had been sunk by the submarine *U98*.

The *Willimantic*, a steamer built in the United States in the First World War, was managed by Lamport and Holt, on behalf of the Ministry of War transport. She was on passage Capetown for Charleston, USA., under the command of Captain Everett, when she was attacked by the submarine *U156*. At the time her chief officer was M. Delaney, and second officer – B.M. Metcalf. The following is the latter's account of the loss.

On June 24, 1942, at 0345 hours we were suddenly attacked by a submarine in position 26N 54W, which opened fire on the surface. First she blew away the wireless room and after end of the chartroom, killing the two radio officers. The next shot blew away the 2.5 in. gun on the poop. I was officer on watch at this time, and the captain tried to keep the submarine astern, but this was difficult because the submarine could not be seen in the darkness, except when she fired her armament. Eventually the ship caught fire amidships, and with shrapnel flying about Captain Everett ordered abandon ship.

The two starboard boats were launched successfully, but the other two were never launched, as a hit was recorded on them whilst they were attempting to put them in the water, killing the third officer, M. Hartley, and an AB; another AB being wounded in the ear.

Captain Everett was taken prisoner on the submarine, and the submarine commander then furnished me with a chart, and having apologised for the sinking of our ship and the deaths of our shipmates, the submarine set off on a North Easterly course, evidently having been on patrol for some time, and being out of torpedoes.

After spreading the boat cover as an awning and rigging up another jury sail, I discussed with the chief officer in the other boat as to his intentions. He decided to steer due West and make for the American coast. I had already decided to make for Antigua, SSW 800 miles, as I thought trying to cross the Gulf Steam was impractical. Mine had the advantage of fair winds and current and estimated I would make it in ten days. He also was of the opinion that they had a better chance of being picked up. I didn't, knowing that in war time ships were routed well away from shipping lanes. After a short discussion I set course SSW and he to the West, but after a while he altered course to the South. We waited until nightfall for him to catch up as he was a few miles behind. (The chief officer's boat landed at St. Kitts, British West Indies, twelve days later).

When darkness fell I decided to carry on. My next day's noon position showed that we were making three knots, and were still on course. We steered by compass during the day and the stars by night. The sail was a dipping lug only, but we fitted an extra jury sail which helped a lot. The wounded AB was attended to, having a piece of shrapnel in his left ear; this was subsequently removed a fortnight later in hospital at Rio de Janeiro.

During the boat passage I rationed the men to one-eighth of a pint of water daily and one meal consisting of corned beef mixed with crushed biscuit, all we had. During the day the men were kept under cover as much as possible, and wet themselves frequently with sea water, in an effort to keep cool.

On the sixth day in the boat, at about 1000 hours we sighted a ship, and having set off flares, noted that the ship was signalling by Aldis – "Proceeding to pick you up", and altered course towards us. The sail was then taken down, and we went alongside in a seamanlike manner, where having boarded, discovered that she was the Norwegian *Tamerlane*, and at first found my legs to be terribly weak after the boat passage. I was greeted by a stewardess who hugged me, and was weeping profusely. Having reported to the master, Captain Kraft, I informed him as to the other boat, which I estimated to be twenty miles or so to the NNE; he agreed to alter course to search for it, but after a while received a message to the effect that there were submarines in the vicinity, he had to abandon the search.

After seven days they were landed at Rio de Janeiro, and subsequently came home aboard the Royal Mail liner *Highland Monarch*.

The next loss was the *Bruyere* on September 23, 1942, when homeward bound from Buenos Aires, she was torpedoed and sunk by *U125* in the approaches to Freetown, fortunately without loss of life. The crew landed at Freetown in the ship's boats. The following day, the *Defoe* which was only two years old caught fire after an explosion had occurred aboard, which was not directly due to enemy action, the bow being blown off up to the foremast. She was abandoned, and sank shortly after. At the time she had been on a voyage from Manchester to Famagusta with drums of liquid chlorine and aeroplane varnish.

The following month the *Laplace* was torpedoed and sunk by the submarine *U159* on October 29, off the South East African coast, while homeward bound from India. The entire crew survived.

The *Browning* was the next vessel of the fleet to be lost. The following account is by Captain B.M. Metcalf.

The *Browning* under the command of Captain I. Sweeney, sailed from Liverpool, light ship for Barrow, in the early hours of October 1, 1942, following extensive repairs in consequence of grounding along with four or five other vessels in convoy, at Belfast Lough, a few months earlier.

At Barrow, she loaded a full military cargo, consisting mainly of ammunition (high explosive shells), tanks, four bulldozers on deck, a large quantity of cased petrol and oil in No. 1 lower hold, and about 100 tons of gelignite and shell fuses in No. 1 'tween deck. Her ballast tanks were thoroughly cleansed and treated, then filled with fresh water.

She eventually sailed from Barrow under sealed orders towards the end of October, joining up with the Liverpool section of a convoy at Liverpool Bay, and later with the Scottish section off Northern Ireland. Altogether there were between fifty and sixty ships. Captain Sweeney of the *Browning* being the Vice-Commodore.

On clearing Northern Ireland, evasive and zig-zag SSW'ly courses were steered under a normal navy escort. The weather being reasonable, a good tight formation was kept, no enemy being sighted, although some occasional depth charging was carried out by the escort, reminding all to be on the alert.

One incident occurred when the chief engineer reported a fracture of about 18 inches in the main intake pipe adjacent to the sea valve, which could be aggravated and prove disastrous in the event of heavy weather and/or extensive depth charging. I was ordered to see if anything could be done, and reported my findings. Whereupon I was told to carry on, and with the assistance of the bosun, carpenter and lamp trimmer, the fractured part of the pipe was paralleled round with burlap strips with a mixture of Stockholm tar and red lead powder, then served tightly round with a one inch wire, and the whole thing was covered with a cement box.

Being under sealed orders, conjecture as to our destination was rife. Some large operation was obvious, rumours spreading thick and fast, and the galley wireless had a rare old time. The captain and I thought North Africa, but when we passed Gibraltar, well to the westward, we gave up surmising. We had steamed about 300 miles southward of the Straits, when we received an Admiralty message to open sealed orders, and learned that the Allied Command were to land at several points on the North African coast. Our destination, the first, being Oran. The message ended to the effect, that this was the start of the Allied offensive and hopefully the turning point of the war, and a large measure of its success depended on the Merchant Service, in whom the command had the utmost confidence.

When darkness fell that night, the convoy turned and headed for a point West of the Straits, which was reached the following night at about 2200 hours. A course was then set East, and the convoy formed into double lines ahead; which must have stretched for at least ten miles. We passed Gibraltar like ghost ships at about midnight and by dawn were all well into the Mediterranean. Apart from an enemy aircraft, nothing else was sighted to give concern; nevertheless all were on the alert and the guns were continuously manned.

At 0800 hours on November 11, the convoy being then 60 miles North of Oran, Captain Sweeney was ordered along with the rest of the Oran section to detach from the main convoy and to commodore the section into Oran. Shortly after, we passed close by the well known passenger ship *Viceroy of India* just as she sank after being torpedoed earlier.

Later a destroyer hailed the *Browning* with instructions to proceed into Arzew Bay, as evidently Oran was not yet clear, the French having put up a lot of resistance. The section anchored in the afternoon, and the *Browning* was boarded by a naval officer, who instructed Captain Sweeney to commodore five other ships into Oran the following day.

The six ships weighed anchor at 1100 hours on November 12, and proceeded double line ahead towards Oran. After rounding the point, course was set South for Oran. Shortly after noon we received orders from the escort to form single line ahead; this was in order to narrow the sweep of the minesweeper ahead, as we were approaching the 100-fathom line.

We were about 12 miles from Oran, when at about 1300 hours there was a violent explosion forward, and the *Browning* shuddered violently, a sheet of flame shot up skywards, and peering through the pall of heavy smoke I could see the foredeck was aflame, the fore topmast was hanging like a donkey's hind leg, the lower mast leaning at a crazy angle to which was attached the 50-ton heavy lift derrick; one bulldozer had gone over the side to port, and the one on the starboard side was hanging over the side by its lashings which had either stretched or carried away. The fore end of the wheel house was blown in against the steering wheel, the helmsman, fortunately, unhurt, was still standing at his post.

The *Browning* was settling fast by the head, and the order was given to abandon ship, whereupon we launched the lifeboats, and in an effort to clear the ship, with the danger of her cargo exploding, we double banked oars. Later being picked up by a corvette, we had left the *Browning* about twenty minutes, when she being well down by the head, there was a heavy explosion, probably from No. 2 hold, but still the old ship stood firm, then followed another, possibly from No. 4 or 5 hold, and finally a third explosion followed after about five minutes by the grandfather of them all, shooting flame and a pall of smoke which ended in a huge ring miles up in the air. The *Browning* had vanished, literally blown to pieces, parts of which were noted falling into the sea over a wide area.

On making a roll call it was learned that a young deck boy was missing; he had been by No. 1 hatch, when the ship had been hit by the torpedo, and had been blown clean over the side.

Eventually being landed at Oran, we subsequently came home aboard the liner *Empress of Scotland*.

Two days after the loss of the *Browning*, the *Lalande* was hit and damaged by the submarine *U73* in position 36.08'N, 03.46'W, but survived and made port. On June 18, 1943 the *Lalande* was again damaged, this time by an aircraft bomb off Cape Espichel, Portugal, but again she was fortunate in making port.

The *Delius* homeward bound from India, was attacked by a glider bomb on November 21, 1943, and was badly damaged. As a result she dropped astern of the convoy, and after great efforts by the crew to control the fire aboard, she managed to rejoin the convoy, and subsequently made port. The attack occurred in position 46.46'N, 18.30'W. The following account was compiled by the ship's carpenter.

Just before dawn on a Friday morning, we left a West of England port, bound for India, in convoy, and on our first Sunday at sea a man was lost overboard. Nobody saw him fall, and it was not until the ship astern put up the signal 'man overboard' that it was noticed that he was missing. Each ship in line threw life belts to him as they passed, but by the time the escort reached the spot, he had disappeared.

From that time onwards it seemed as though we had a hoodoo on board; nothing seemed to go right, even the food went bad as the refrigeration went wrong; however nothing else happened until we got into the Indian Ocean. It was at the end of the monsoon season and the weather was very hot when the chief steward was taken ill; after three days of lingering with this illness, which we took to be simply the effects of the heat, he appeared on deck at about 5 o'clock in the morning, lay down in a hammock that was stretched on the boat deck, and died. We were all shocked at this, and began to think that it really was an unlucky trip. We buried him at sea, and those readers who have seen a burial at sea, will agree with me when I say, that it was a very solemn occasion. We carried on from there to our port of discharge in India, and there our bad luck showed itself again.

All hands on board, with very few exceptions, fell ill with malaria or dysentery, or both. We managed to get over it however, and started for home again, wondering what else was in store for us. We were not left waiting long, because we had hardly arrived at the Suez Canal when the chief officer fell ill, and took to his bunk. On arrival at Port Said he was so bad it was decided to put him ashore to hospital. Little did we know that we would not see him again, for four hours after being admitted to hospital he died.

So we left Egypt minus three of our original crew, and fully convinced that fate was not on our side. We safely passed through the Mediterranean and out into the Atlantic Ocean. We had barely got clear of Gibraltar however, when a single enemy plane came out, and commenced to circle the convoy. Keeping well out of range of our guns. Each night he would go away; but the following morning he was back. The fact that he did not attack us convinced us that he was only acting as a spotter for other planes or submarines. After some days like this, it was noted on one day that the 'plane was not to be seen. So we decided that this was the day for our final piece of bad luck.

Sure enough at about 3.15 pm the aircraft warning sounded and we all took up our stations. Being the ship's carpenter, I was in the repair party, and so I took up my station with the bosun on the boat deck. About nine 'planes came out and most of these got through to the convoy. They first attacked a ship that had dropped astern of the convoy a short distance, owing to some engine trouble; they dropped about ten bombs, of which only one scored a hit, but unfortunately that one was enough to sink her.

After this the *Delius* became the target, and as a bomber came towards us from the direction of the stern quarter, a strange thing happened. A small plane appeared to drop from the rear of the bomber, and gathering speed all the time, flew over the top of the bombers, circled and came at us. We were taken completely by surprise, and thought it was an RAF fighter that had come to protect us. However, as it appeared to be making straight for us, we decided to take no chances, and our gunners fired at it, and scoring a direct hit, it exploded near the ship.

Then it dawned on us that this was Jerry's secret weapon, that we had heard rumours about, and was called a "shelic bomb". The advantage of this new bomb for the enemy, is that the parent 'plane can keep out of range of our guns, and direct his shelic bomb by radio control to whichever target he wishes. This he did to us, after we exploded the first bomb. He flew past and went towards another ship, launched his bomb, which turned around and came back at us.

As I said earlier, I was on the boat deck with the bosun, and with us was an ordinary seaman, and behind us was a gunner. As I saw the bomb coming I shouted to the others to take cover, and dived for a door leading into the funnel, which was the nearest cover available. I had hardly got there with these two seamen when the bomb landed on the foredeck.

I could not move forward or back, but just stood swaying from side to side; the blast hit us from one side then the other, and we saw all kinds of sparks, lumps of wood, metal, and a thick cloud of smoke go past us on the deck. I could not quite realise that we had been hit until I saw that the bosun was badly wounded, and the gunner was staggering around holding his stomach.

The bosun died while I was with him, and after seeing the gunner was being cared for by the first aid party, I went to the foredeck where the lamp trimmer was trying to put out the fire caused by the bomb when it struck No. 3 hold. He was throwing burning bags and pieces of tarpaulin over the side, and after a few minutes we thought that everything was out. Then we saw smoke coming from another hole and we went to investigate, having been joined by other men by this time.

We discovered that it was just smoke coming along the top of the cargo in the shelter deck, so we commenced to cover up again. As we were doing so jerry came back again and we all tried to find some hole to crawl into for protection, but he was only taking photographs of his handiwork, so we were all right.

We got back amidships to find that besides the bosun, our captain, a steward and an AB had been killed, while quite a number of others were injured.

We sent out a call for a doctor, and shortly afterwards one was transferred aboard. I would like to say here how very good and sympathetic the naval escorts were to us. Every so often a corvette would come as close as possible and ask us if there was anything we needed, and they supplied us with hoses, medical stores, and even cigarettes.

That night we discovered that a piece of hot shrapnel had gone down a ventilator to the lower hold and the cotton which was stowed there was on fire. So a few of us stood all night, pumping water down the ventilator in a vain effort to extinguish the fire. Next morning came the job of burying our dead. I mentioned before how solemn it is to witness a burial at sea. Imagine it as we watched four of our shipmates, one after the other, go into the sea; men who just a few hours earlier had been very much alive.

Later we took on board three officers from the ship that had been sunk previously; they had volunteered to come on board to help us when they heard that we had only one officer left. And were they a help to us? Right here, I thank God for men like them, who, although they themselves had lost everything when their own ship was sunk, volunteered to go to the help of other comrades who needed help. They cheered us up with their wisecracks and jokes, and at that time we needed their support, because besides the fire we discovered that the water we were pumping into the hold was lodging on the starboard side of the ship and was giving the ship a very bad list.

To make matters worse, a heavy sea came up which held the ship further over. It was so bad that none of us on board thought that she would right herself each time she rolled over. We were expecting her to turn right over, and had that happened not one of us would have been saved. The water in the hold had now penetrated into the steward's stores, entry into which was possible from the main deck.

So we started the portable pumps going to try and pump the water away and to right the ship. The trouble was that the cargo of peanuts in the hold was floating round in the stores and kept getting into the sucker of the pump, stopping the water from going out. As a result at least one of us had to stay down there all the time to keep the suction clear. Some of us were down there at least eight hours at a time. So we carried on for the rest of the voyage, 1,000 miles to go, and the ship on fire with a very serious list to starboard, and with injured men on board.

At times the ship fell back from the convoy, but eventually managed to catch up and keep her station. The engineers, in an effort to save her, drilled holes in the bulkhead between the engine room and No. 3 hold, through which they pumped steam to help control the fire.

In spite of all this we managed to get the ship into a British port. We had no compasses, no degaussing gear, the steering gear was faulty and two of the six cylinders of the engine were out of action. The ship was steered by the stars at night while making port.

I would like to point out that the bringing home of this ship from the point where we were bombed was entirely due to the 28 year old second mate, who was the only officer we had left. On the death of the chief officer he took over the job; and when the captain died he took over the captain's position in command. It was owing to his endurance and good spirits that we were able to carry on.

To give an example, owing to the fact that the dining saloon was wrecked the officers and engineers had to take their meals in the P.O.'s mess, and the table was only meant for six men. Imagine the sight of eighteen men eating in there. It was a common sight to see the officer in command of the ship, sitting on the deck with his plate on his knees, while apprentices and junior engineers were sitting at the table.

We moored at the salvage berth and the Salvage and National Fire Service personnel came on board to take over the job from us. It was a relief to us because for the whole five and a half days we were trying to control the fire, some of us had had no more than five hours sleep per day. We were much amused when the NFS sealed up the stores where we had spent so many hours because, they said, there was a danger of fumes from the peanuts going bad.

Our injured went to hospital, together with men suffering from shock. Two men died in hospital from their injuries, making a total loss of personnel of nine men, including the three prior to the bombing attack.

Our three friends, the officers from the ship that had sunk, left for their homes and sent us a telegram with best wishes, adding, "never were so many peanuts eaten by so few". It took us over a week to get the fire aboard the ship under control and it was ten days before we finally docked at Glasgow.

As a result of this ordeal, and for their actions in bringing the *Delius* home, a number of the crew were decorated and commended. A list of such decorations appears elsewhere in these pages.

The last war loss suffered by the company was the *Devis* on July 5, 1943, when she was the commodore ship of a convoy taking part in the invasion of Sicily. She was torpedoed and sunk by the German submarine *U593* in position 37.01'N, 04.10'E. Although none of the crew were lost, she was carrying a large number of troops and there were heavy casualties amongst them. Her valuable cargo of tanks and other equipment was a loss in the subsequent action to take Sicily.

On March 6, 1945 the *Empire Geraint*, managed by Lamport and Holt Line on behalf of the Ministry of War Transport, and under the command of Captain A.R. Bibby, was torpedoed off Milford Haven, by the submarine *U775*, but was subsequently towed into port, repaired, eventually joining the fleet as the *Millais*, the same year.

After the fall of Poland three Polish passenger liners were placed under the management of the company by the Ministry of War Transport and became troopships, running principally to the Far East and India. These were the *Pulaski* of 1912, *Kosciuszko* of 1915 and the 14,287 ton *Batory* of 1936, which was a fast modern liner. All three kept their Polish crews throughout the war, but carried a Lamport and Holt master as liaison officer. At the conclusion of hostilities the *Batory* was handed back to Poland but the crews of the other two ships refused to be repatriated and the vessels were placed under the British flag and their crews signed British articles. They became the *Empire Penryn* and *Empire Helford* respectively and remained under the company's management until they were eventually sold for demolition. Similar arrangements were in being in respect of a number of other vessels of various nationalities. Two Belgian ships, which were taken over by the Ministry at the end of hostilities as troopships, becoming the *Empire Bure* and *Empire Test*, were also managed for a similar period.

During the entire period of hostilities Lamport and Holt were the Liverpool agents for the United States Maritime Commission and handled all their ships using the port.

The Polish liner *Batory* (14,287 gross tons) was managed by the Lamport & Holt Line for the early part of the Second World War. *(Skyfotos Ltd.)*

The Polish liner *Kosciuszko* of 1913 was managed throughout the war. Following hostilities she was renamed *Empire Helford*, the company continuing to manage her until the 1950s.
(T. Rayner)

The former Belgian vessel, *Empire Bure* became a troopship and was managed by the company. *(T. Rayner)*

The troopship *Empire Test*, a former Belgian owned vessel, was managed on behalf of the Government. *(T. Rayner)*

A number of other ships were managed during the war, including the *Empire Ibex* of 1918, *Empire Franklyn* of 1941, *Empire Dynasty* of 1944, *Samana, Samariz, Samarovsk,* and *Samur,* all of 1943, *Empire Bardolph* of 1943 and *Empire Geraint* of 1942. Of these the *Empire Geraint, Empire Bardolph* and *Samariz* were to be purchased under the ship disposal scheme of the British Government, becoming the *Millais, Memling* and *Lassell.*

Harland and Wolff Ltd., Belfast delivered two replacement 'D' class ships for those lost; they were the *Devis* in 1944 and *Defoe* in 1945, both taking the names of the ships they replaced.

The service between New York, Brazil and the River Plate was, during the war years, maintained entirely by chartered neutral tonnage.

The *Empire Ibex* was lost as the result of a collision with an aircraft carrier on July 1, 1943. The ship at first remained afloat, but had to be abandoned on July 2 and finally sank a day later, in position 53.36'N, 36.16'W, while under the command of Captain Sweeney, who was in no way responsible for the loss.

A number of other actions took place involving Lamport and Holt ships which are worthy of note. The *Sheridan* had a number of narrow misses during the war; on one occasion in the North Sea a German 'plane dropped a bomb so close that it caused a leak in one of the double bottom tanks. The ship carried on but was eventually drydocked for repairs at Montevideo. On another occasion, while in a homeward bound convoy from Freetown, a submarine surfaced nearby at night and fired a torpedo at the *Sheridan* which took avoiding action; the torpedo missed her but unfortunately claimed another ship in the convoy as victim. The *Sheridan,* being somewhat slow, on more than one occasion fell back, being unable to keep up with a convoy, but survived the war in spite of this.

The following report was made to the naval authorities at Bone, in respect of the success of the *Delane's* A.A. barrage while lying at that port between December 12-17, 1942.

> Under continuous air attacks every night while the *Delane* was alongside the wharf at Bone, it can definitely be stated that the security of the ship was dependent on the immediate readiness for use of all the machine guns attached to the vessel, namely four Oerlions, two Marlins and two Hotchkiss. The way these were manned by the naval and military personnel no doubt, together with the barrage set up by the other vessels in port, protected the number of British merchant ships from being damaged by enemy aircraft.
>
> On Saturday night and Sunday morning of December 12-13 respectively eight enemy 'planes were estimated to have been over the port, five of which were destroyed, three only being claimed by the RAF night fighters, full credit being given to the *Delane* for the destruction of the fourth, and part credit for the crashing of the remaining aircraft was also given to the same vessel.
>
> On the night of December 13, when the port was again attacked by enemy aircraft, the ack-ack barrage of the ship was so intense that the only visible 'plane was immediately engaged while making a dive bombing attack on this particular vessel, and the 20 mm. bullets of the Oerlikon gun fitted on the port side of the boat deck were seen to pierce the 'plane, she was unable to recover from the dive and her remnants were observed the following morning on the opposite side of the harbour amongst civilian property. The position of where the plane crashed was in a direct line from the *Delane,* where she was last observed by the gunners.
>
> (Signed) E. Evans – Armament Officer
> G.E. Roberts – Master

The *Samarovsk* under the command of Captain D. C. Roberts, while taking part in the Normandy landings, and subsequently supply, claimed a direct hit during this period, parts of the offending plane falling on the deck of the vessel.

During 1943, while crossing the North Atlantic Westbound from London (North about) to New York, the *Balfe* encountered bad weather and, being in ballast, a jury staysail was rigged to help the ship steer; an unusual occurrence for a steamer of this period.

During the period of hostilities a large number of loyal men died whilst serving aboard the company's ships as a result of enemy action. Fifty of the company's seagoing personnel were decorated or received official commendations in recognition of their efforts, as follows:

Name	Rank	Award
Barton, H.	Chief Officer	MBE
Beattie, J.	Chief Engineer	Commended
Bell, R.C.	Ordinary Seaman	BEM
Bibby, AR.	Captain	OBE

Brazill, L.	Radio Officer	Commended
Byrne, G.F.	Captain	OBE
Conlan, R.J.	Boatswain	BEM
Crapper, E.G.	Second Engineer	Commended
Crowe, J.S.	Second Officer	Commended
Davis, V.	Chief Steward	BEM
Denson, W.	Captain	OBE
Edwards, E.	Boatswain	BEM
Filshie, G.	Chief Engineer	OBE
Geddes, A.	Fourth Engineer	Commended
George, J.H.	Captain	OBE
Gill, J.	Boatswain	BEM
Griffiths, F.A.	Chief Officer	Commended
Hughes, A.	Captain	Commended
Jermyn, E.L.	Chief Officer	MBE
Johnstone, J.	Junior Engineer	Commended
Jones, M.	Chief Steward	BEM
Large, F.W.	Ordinary Seaman	Commended
Little, J.A.	Captain	OBE
Loynds, D.	Fifth Engineer	Commended
MacKellar, A.	Captain	Commended
Major, T.	Captain	Commended
Marshall, G.	Chief Officer	OBE
McPherson, D.	Third Officer	Commended
Merrett, G.C.	Cook	BEM
Metcalf, B.	Chief Officer	Commended
Nye, K.B.K.	Radio Officer	Commended
Owen, I.	Chief Officer	MBE
Page, F.J.	Able Seaman	BEM
Penhale, J.E.	Cadet	Commended
Philpott, A.R.	Carpenter	BEM
Preston, B.	Deck Boy	Mentioned in Despatches
Purton, C.G.	Captain	OBE
Reid, J.	Carpenter	BEM
Roberts, D.C.	Captain	OBE
Roberts, G.E.	Captain	OBE
Roberts, M.C.	Cadet	Commended
Rogers, J.A.	Lamp Trimmer	BEM
Rutherford, W.B.	Chief Engineer	MBE
Scott, G.	Captain	Commended
Teunon, F.G.S.	Chief Engineer	Commended
Toy	Chief Steward	Polish Government Award
Underhill, H.W.	Chief Officer	MBE
Watson, A.	Captain	OBE and Polish Government Award
Wood, R.G.	Boatswain	BEM
Williams, S.M.	Second Officer	Commended

The managing director of Lamport and Holt Line during this period had designed a lifeboat for use in the company's ships, which was later to be adopted by the Ministry of War Transport and which provided more than the usual amount of shelter to the boat's occupants. The following is an extract from the *Evening Express* for January 27, 1944

LIFE-BOAT FOR 55 SAVED 84

A "Lowe" ship's life-boat – of the type constructed to carry fifty-five persons and described by Ministry of War Transport shipping experts as the safest in the world – has brought eighty-four men to safety.

Mr. Francis H. Lowe, Managing Director of the Lamport and Holt Line, Liverpool, inventor of the life-boat, told the "Evening Express" today that even with eighty-four men aboard the life-boat was by no means near a sinking condition.

This life-boat, which will soon be part of the equipment of all British and Allied merchant ships, had to be launched against a head sea when a British ship was sunk.

The boat was launched much more easily than was expected in such a sea and then came the problem of taking off the crew, eighty-four in a boat built for fifty-five seemed to be asking even too much of the latest life-boat. But they got in and, although cramped and uncomfortable, their extra weight did not adversely affect the seaworthiness of the life-boat.

Some hours later a British destroyer spotted the boat and took the men aboard.

Mr. Lowe spent three years in experimenting before the first boat was finally ready for Ministry of War Transport tests.

He personally bore all expenses – and today stated that he has given the life-boat's secrets to Britain and her Allies. "I have not taken out any patent rights and do not intend doing so", he said, "When something is produced which will save life at sea I think it should be available to all men".

FLEET LIST Part 8

Name & Period in Fleet	Gross tons	History
Defoe (1) 1940-1942	6,245	Motorship. 1940 built by Harland & Wolff Ltd., Belfast, for Lamport & Holt Line Ltd.; 1941 re-measured and tonnage increased; 24.9.1942 abandoned on fire following an explosion on board, South West of Rockall, and subsequently sank; not due to enemy action.

The launch of the first *Defoe* by Harland & Wolff Ltd., Belfast, in 1940. She was lost in 1942, but not due to enemy action.   *(Harland & Wolff Ltd.)*

Name & Period in Fleet	Gross tons	History
Debrett 1940-1955 1956-1964	6,244	Motorship. 1940 built by Harland & Wolff Ltd., Belfast, for Lamport & Holt Line Ltd.; 1942 re-measured, tonnage increased to 8,104 gross; 1955 bareboat chartered to Blue Star Line Ltd., renamed *Washington Star*; 1956 charter ended, renamed *Debrett*; 1964 to Embajada Cia. Nav. S.A., renamed *Ambasciata*; 28.12.1964 arrived at Osaka for breaking up.

The *Debrett* at war.
  (A. Duncan)

The *Debrett* in the English Channel.
(*Skyfotos Ltd.*)

Having spent over a week in Santos Roads the *Debrett* is shown leaving the anchorage on her way to enter the port of Santos, Brazil in 1962.

(P.M. Heaton)

Name & Period in Fleet	Gross tons	History
Devis (2) 1944-1955 1956-1962	8,187	Motorship. 1944 built by Harland & Wolff Ltd., Belfast, for Lamport & Holt Line Ltd.; 1955 bareboat chartered to Blue Star Line Ltd., renamed *Oakland Star*; 1956 charter ended, renamed *Devis*; 4.7.1962 arrived at Spezia for breaking up.

The *Devis* (2) in the English Channel. *(Skyfotos Ltd.)*

Name & Period in Fleet	Gross tons	History
Defoe (2) 1945-1954 1958-1966	8,462	Motorship. 1945 built by Harland & Wolff Ltd., Belfast, for Lamport & Holt Line Ltd.; 1954 to Blue Star Line Ltd., renamed *Geelong Star*; 1958 bareboat chartered to Lamport & Holt Line Ltd., renamed *Defoe*; 1966 to Astrofeliz Cia. Nav. S.A., Panama, renamed *Argolis Star*; 1967 to Argolis Shipping Co. S.A., Piraeus; 29.10.1969 arrived at Shanghai for breaking up.

The *Defoe* (2). *(Skyfotos Ltd.)*

10. THE IMMEDIATE POST-WAR FLEET

Towards the end of the Second World War a number of organisations cast their eyes towards Lamport and Holt Line Ltd., as a very desirable and asset-laden company well worth acquiring. In the Spring of 1944 United Molasses had offered up to 23/6 (in cash and shares) for each 6/8 Lamport and Holt share. Following this Blue Star Line Ltd on behalf of Frederick Leyland and Co. Ltd offered 25/- per share, which in June, 1944 was accepted by over 85% of shareholders, and thus the company thereafter came under the control of the Vestey group. A new management was formed, only Mr. Lowe of the former directors remaining with the company. He became the first General Manager, a post he held until his retirement in 1952, although he continued as a director until his death in 1975.

At the conclusion of the war Lamport & Holt owned nine ships and in addition there were four troopships being managed by the company, together with a number of cargo ships yet to be returned to the Ministry of War Transport.

The first acquisitions after the war were two steamers of 7,000 gross tons from the Ministry, the *Empire Bardolph* and *Empire Geraint* which became the *Memling* and *Millais* respectively, both useful ships having a limited amount of refrigerated space, and in 1945 two other 'D' class ships, the *Debrett* and *Devis* (2) were returned to the Belfast yard of their builders, Harland and Wolff Ltd., for part of their cargo space to be converted for the carriage of refrigerated cargo.

The following year two more ships were added to the fleet. One was the large *Empire Haig*, which was renamed *Dryden*; she was a most useful ship of almost 10,000 gross tons. The second vessel acquired was the *Celtic Star* (ex-*Empire Galahad*), the first transfer from Blue Star Line, instances of which were to be commonplace from then onwards. This ship became the Lamport and Holt *Murillo*.

A significant event in 1946 occurred when the Vestey Group gained control of the Booth Steamship Co. Ltd., also of Liverpool. Both Booth and Lamport & Holt retained their own offices, staff – both seagoing and shore based – and their own ships. Thereafter a number of inter-company transfers took place, prior to newbuildings arriving in the Lamport & Holt Line fleet.

During 1947 a new company was registered at Panama City under the title of Panama Shipping Corp. Inc. with the intention of owning and chartering to Lamport & Holt and Booth Line vessels registered in Panama. These were ships which traded from New York to Brazil, the Amazon, West Indies and the River Plate, and were manned by West Indian and Brazilian crews, a practice used for many years. The masters, mates and engineers as before were sent out normally as passengers to join these ships, which rarely returned to the U.K. In the event two American built 'Victory' ships were bareboat chartered by Panama Shipping in that year from the United States Maritime Commission and demise chartered by them to Lamport & Holt. These were named *Vianna* and *Villar* of 7,602 gross tons and were operated from 1947 until returned to the USMC in 1949. It was found that they were too big for the company's requirements, but were granted 'packet Boat' status in the River Plate.

FLEET LIST Part 9

Name & Period in Fleet	Gross tons	History
Memling (3) 1945-1953 1957-1959	7,017	Steamship. 1943 built by Short Bros. Ltd., Sunderland, as *Empire Bardolph* for Ministry of War Transport (Donaldson Line); 1945 to Lamport & Holt Line Ltd., renamed *Memling*; 1953 to Blue Star Line Ltd., renamed *Vancouvier Star*; 1957 to Lamport & Holt Line Ltd., renamed *Memling*; 1957 to Blue Star Line Ltd., bareboat chartered to Lamport & Holt Ltd.; 23.10.1959 arrived at Flushing for breaking up.
Millais (2) 1945-1952	7,001	Steamship. 1942 built by C. Connell and Co. Ltd., Glasgow, as *Empire Geraint* for Ministry of War Transport (Royal Mail Lines Ltd.); 1945 management transferred to Lamport & Holt Line Ltd. 1945 to Lamport & Holt Line., renamed *Millais*; 1952 to Blue Star Line Ltd., renamed *Oregon Star*; 1954 to Iris Shipping and Trading Corp., Monrovia, renamed *Captayannis*; 1960 to Paleocrassis Bros., Piraeus; 28.2.1962 grounded near Goree Lightship, while inbound for Rotterdam; badly damaged; 1962 broken up by F. Rijsdyk, Hendrik-ido-Ambacht.

Built in 1943 as the *Empire Bardolph*, the *Memling* (3) was acquired in 1945.

(*A. Duncan*)

Formerly the *Empire Geraint* of 1942, the *Millais* (2) was purchased in 1945.

(*World Ship Photo Library*)

Name & Period in Fleet	Gross tons	History
Dryden (3) 1946-1952 *Devis* (3) 1963-1969	9,942	Motorship. 1944 built by Lithgows Ltd., Port Glasgow, as *Empire Haig* for Ministry of War Transport (Ellerman Wilson Line); 1946 to Lamport & Holt Line Ltd., renamed *Dryden*; 1952 to Blue Star Line Ltd., renamed *Fremantle Star*; 1956 renamed *Catalina Star*; 1963 bareboat chartered to Lamport & Holt Line Ltd., renamed *Devis*; 1966 to Lamport & Holt Line Ltd.; 1969 to Bry Overseas Nav. Inc., renamed *Mondia*; 23.12.1969 arrived Kaohsiung for breaking up by Han Tai Iron and Steel Company.

The *Dryden* (3) served the company as such from 1946 to 1952.

(*A. Duncan*)

The *Dryden* (3) returned to Lamport & Holt in 1963 but under the name *Devis* (3).
(A. Duncan)

Name & Period in Fleet	Gross tons	History
Murillo (2) 1946-1952	7,046	Steamship. 1942 built by Lithgows Ltd., Port Glasgow, as *Empire Galahad* for Ministry of War Transport (Blue Star Line Ltd.); 1946 to Blue Star Line Ltd., renamed *Celtic Star*; 1946 to Lamport & Holt Line Ltd., renamed *Murillo*; 1952 to Industriale Maritime S.p.A., Genoa, renamed *Bogliasco*; 1963 to Ocean Shipping and Enterprises S.A., Panama, renamed *Ocean Peace*; 13.9.1967 arrived at Kaohsiung for breaking up.
George Salt 1946	77	Motor tug. 1936 built by Henry Robb Ltd., Leith, as *George Salt* for Blackfriars Lighterage and Cartage Co. Ltd. (Blue Star Line Ltd.); 1936 to Frederick Leyland and Co. Ltd. (Blue Star Line Ltd.); 1946 to Lamport & Holt Line Ltd.; 1946 to Cia. Nav. das Lagaos, Rio Grande do Sul; 1948 renamed *Sao Cristovao;* 1970 no further details.

The tug *George Salt* was bought by Lamport & Holt Line in 1946, and sent out to Rio Grande do Sul where she was renamed *Sao Cristovao*. Carrying the company's funnel colours; and flying the Lamport & Holt houseflag with the letters CNL thereon. The tug is shown in 1963. *(P.M. Heaton)*

Name & Period in Fleet	Gross tons	History

Sheridan (2)
1947-1960

3,827

Motorship. 1945 built by Consolidated Steep Corp., Wilmington, California, as *Hickory Glen* for United States Maritime Commission, and baseboat chartered to Ministry of War Transport (China Nav. Co. Ltd.); 1947 returned to United States Maritime Commission; 1947 to Lamport & Holt Line Ltd., renamed *Sheridan*; 1960 to Austasia Line Ltd., Singapore, renamed *Matupi*; 1964 to Kie Hock Shipping (Hong Kong) Co. Ltd., Hong Kong, renamed *Tong Lam*; 1968 to Asia Selatan Enterprises Ltd., 1970 to Sakota Ltda. S.A., Panama; 27.10.1970 aground on Scarborough Reef, 420 miles North West of Manila, broke in three and became a total loss, while on passage North Korea to Chittagong with a cargo of pig iron.

Lassell (3)
1947-1962

7,256

Steamship. 1943 built by Bethlehem Fairfield Shipyard Inc., Baltimore, as *John J. McGraw* for United States Maritime Commission; 1943 bareboat chartered to Ministry of War Transport (Lamport & Holt Line Ltd.), renamed *Samariz*; 1944 renamed *John J. McGraw*; 1947 to Lamport & Holt Line Ltd., renamed *Lassell*; 1962 to Poseidon Cia. Nav. S.A., Beirut, renamed *Alolos II*; 1967 to Falcon Shipping Company, Cyprus; 1968 broken up at Shanghai.

The Liberty ship *Lassell* (3) in the English Channel.
(Skyfotos Ltd.)

The *Lassell* (3).
(A. Duncan)

Name & Period in Fleet	Gross tons	History
Byron (2) 1947-1953 *Lalande* (4) 1953-1961	6,902	Steamship. 1940 built by Barclay, Curle and Co. Ltd., Glasgow as *Empire Voice* for Ministry of War Transport (British India Steam Navigation Co. Ltd.); 1946 to Booth Steamship Co. Ltd., renamed *Bernard*; 1947 to Lamport & Holt Ltd., renamed *Byron*; 1953 renamed *Lalande*; 1961 to Wm. Brandt, Sons and Company, renamed *Uncle Bart*; 8.9.1961 arrived at Moji for breaking up.

Joining the fleet in 1947 as the *Byron* (2), the vessel is shown as the *Lalande* (4) which she was renamed in 1953.

(*A. Duncan*)

Name & Period in Fleet	Gross tons	History
Vianna 1947-1949	7,602	Steamship. 1945 built by Bethlehem Fairfield Shipyard Inc., Baltimore, as *Atlantic City Victory* for United States Maritime Commission; 1947 demise chartered to Panama Shipping Corp. Inc., and operated by Lamport & Holt Line Ltd., renamed *Vianna*; 1949 returned to United States Maritime Commission; 1949 to Cie. Royale Belge-Argentine S.A., Antwerp, renamed *Flandres*; 1962 to China Union Lines Ltd, Keelung, renamed *Taipei Victory*; 1974 broken up in Taiwan.

The Victory ship *Vianna* on charter from the Panama Shipping Corporation from 1947.

Name & Period in Fleet	Gross tons	History
Villar 1947-1949	7,607	Steamship. 1945 built by Permanente Metals Corp., Richmond, California, as *El Reno Victory* for United States Maritime Commission; 1947 demise chartered to Panama Shipping Corp. Inc., and operated by Lamport & Holt Line Ltd., renamed *Villar*; 1949 returned to United States Maritime Commission; 1949 to Koninklijke Nederlandsche Stoomboot Maatschappij K.N.S.M. Netherlands, renamed *Bennekom*; 1966 to Ithacamar Cia. de Nav., Monrovia, renamed *Ithaka Victory*; 1968 to Venus Maritime Corp. Monrovia, renamed *Venus Victory*; 1970 broken up at Kaohsiung.
Bronte (2) 1948-1950	4,949	Steamship. 1930 built by Cammell Laird and Co. Ltd., Birkenhead, as *Benedict* for Booth Steamship Co. Ltd.; 1948 to Lamport & Holt Line Ltd., renamed *Bronte*; 1950 to Muzaffer Necati Pehlivan, Istanbul, renamed *Muzaffer*; 1957 to Riza ve Aslan Sadikoglu Ortaklari Komandity, Istanbul, renamed *Umran*; 14.2.1961 arrived at Vigo for breaking up.

The *Bronte* (2).   (A. Duncan)

Browning (2) 1949-1951	4,862	Steamship. 1928 built by R. & W. Hawthorn, Leslie and Co. Ltd., Hebburn, as *Boniface* for Booth Steamship Co. Ltd.; 1949 to Lamport & Holt Line Ltd., renamed *Browning*; 1951 to Cia de Nav. Niques, Panama, renamed *Sannicola*; 1951 to Muko Kisen K.K., Japan, renamed *Mizuho Maru*; 28.2.1961 arrived at Mukaishima for breaking up.

Name & Period in Fleet	Gross tons	History
Spenser (3) 1950-1955 *Roscoe* 1955-1962	6,334	Motorship. 1935 built by Bremer Vulkan, Vegesack, as *Dusseldorf* for Norddeutseier Lloyd, Germany; 25.12.1939 captured off the Chilean Coast by HMS *Despatch*; 1940 placed under the Ministry of War Transport, renamed *Poland*; 1940 renamed *Empire Confidence*; 1946 to Alexandria Steam Navigation Co. Ltd., Liverpool, renamed *Star of El Nil*; 1949 to Ministry of War Transport; 1950 to Lamport & Holt Line Ltd., renamed *Spenser*; 1955 renamed *Roscoe*; 1962 broken up at Bilbao.

The *Spenser* (3) was acquired for the New York, Brazil and River Plate service in 1950. In 1955 she was transferred to the UK and renamed *Roscoe*. Shown at Brooklyn in December, 1957.

(F.W. Hawks)

Another view of the *Roscoe* at Brooklyn.
(World Ship Photo Library)

The *Roscoe* in the English Channel.   *(Skyfotos Ltd.)*

Name & Period in Fleet	Gross tons	History
Lalande (3) 1951	7,219	Steamship. 1944 built by Bethlehem Fairfield Shipyard Inc., Baltimore, as *Samnid* for United States Maritime Commission, and bareboat chartered to the Ministry of War Transport. (Blue Star Line Ltd.); 1946 to Blue Star Line Ltd., renamed *Pacific Star*; 1951 to Lamport & Holt Line Ltd., renamed *Lalande*; 1951 to Soc. Anon. Importazione Carbon e Nav., Italy, renamed *Ninfea*; 1959 to China Ocean Shipping Company, Shanghai, renamed *Nan Hai 147*; 1979 renamed *Hong QI 147*; 1980s no further details.
Sallust (2) 1951-1958	2,993	Steamship. 1948 built by Wm. Pickersgill and Sons Ltd., Sunderland, as *Dunstan* for Booth Steamship Co. Ltd.; 1951 to Lamport & Holt Line Ltd., renamed *Sallust;* 1958 to Booth Steamship Co. Ltd., renamed *Dunstan*; 1966 renamed *Basil*; 1968 to Cia. Mtma. Viahoulis S.A., Panama, renamed *Christina*; 3.1.1969 caught fire at Galveston; 1969 broken up at Barranquilla.

The *Sallust* (2).
(World Ship Photo Library)

Name & Period in Fleet	Gross tons	History
Tapajos 1951-1955	2,877	Steamship. 1944 built by Foundation Maritime Ltd., Picton, Nova Scotia as *Liscomb Park* for Park Steamship Co. Ltd., Montreal; 1945 to Seagull Steamship Co. Ltd., Montreal; 1948 renamed *Saint Malo*; 1951 to Panama Shipping Corp. Inc., bareboat chartered to Lamport & Holt Line Ltd., renamed *Tapajos*; 1955 to A/S Auctor; (Arnt Haarberg), Bergen, renamed *Orland*; 1964 to Cia. de Nav. Fortitudo Lines S.A., Monrovia; renamed *Sagitta*; 1964 to Cia de Nav. Pintamar S.A., Monrovia, renamed *Sfinge*; 1966 to Cia de Nav. General, Monrovia; 1969 to Somali Republic register; renamed *Sirio*; 1971 renamed *Suerte*; 18.5.1972 arrived at Trieste for breaking up.
Laplace (3) 1952-1953	7,283	Steamship. 1944 built by New England Shipbuilding Corp., Portland, Maine, as *Samannan* for United States Maritime Commission, bareboat chartered to Ministry of War Transport (Blue Star Line Ltd); 1946 to Blue Star Line Ltd.; 1947 renamed *Oregon Star*; 1952 to Lamport & Holt Line Ltd., renamed *Laplace*; 1953 to San Panteleimon Cia. Nav. S.A., Panama, renamed *San Panteleimon*; 20.4.1967 arrived at Yokosuka for breaking up.

11. NEW SHIPS JOIN THE FLEET

Following the incorporation of both Lamport & Holt Line and the Booth Steamship Company in the Vestey Group at the end of or shortly after the war, a heavy rebuilding programme was commenced in respect of both Blue Star Line and Booth, and for the next few years as those vessels were completed, all surplus tonnage had either been sold out of the group or transferred to Lamport & Holt, as something of a stop gap for them. However, during 1952, the long awaited new ships for the Lamport & Holt Line began to arrive. During this year a steamer and two motorships were delivered to their order. The *Romney*, a turbine steamer of 8,237 gross tons, built by Cammell Laird and Co. Ltd., Birkenhead, became the company's flagship, a position she held for twenty-six years. A motorship of similar tonnage, the *Raeburn* was delivered by Harland and Wolff Ltd., Belfast. Both these ships were designed for service between the United Kingdom and Brazil and the River Plate. The other ship was the 4,459 gross ton *Siddons* which came from the Sunderland yard of William Pickersgill and Sons Ltd for the trade from New York to Brazil and the River Plate. However on September 3, 1953 the *Raeburn* grounded on Monkstone Rocks in the Bristol Channel near Cardiff, and took some time to refloat, Bottom damage was so severe that it took almost a year for her builders to repair her at Belfast.

Secondhand ships continued to arrive, but a further 'R' class ship, the *Raphael* was delivered in 1953, designed for the UK – River Plate trade. A motorship of 7,971 gross tons, built by Bartram and Sons Ltd., Sunderland, she was the fastest ship launched at that yard to that date, and the fastest in the Lamport & Holt fleet, achieving $17\frac{1}{2}$ knots on her trials. These 'R' class vessels, although all different, were to be some of the most outstanding, in terms of lines, ever to join the fleet.

The following figures give some idea of the size of the fleet over the years up until 1953:

Year	No. of Ships	Total Gross Tonnage
1875	31	48,236
1888	50	93,331
1890	59	109,493
1894	49	100,731
1914	36	198,992
1924	50	322,857
1936	21	144,062
1939	21	141,003
1945	9	65,396
1953	16	105,970

As can be seen the fleet had made a good recovery by 1953 and was approaching the strength at which it had entered the war in 1939. Another interesting point revealed is that the number of ships owned in 1953 as compared with the 1890s had dropped to less than a third, while the tonnage overall in 60 years had been maintained with the increased size of individual ships.

The year 1953 is a good one to study the breakdown of the fleet into trades and groups of ships. There were still five 'D' class ships, three of which had refrigerated space, and the *Dryden* which was also so equipped; two 'L' class and three modern 'R' class ships, all being general cargo ships. Of these most were engaged on the United Kingdom to Brazil and River Plate trades, although occasionally over the previous few years a 'D' class ship was to be seen in New Zealand, having been time-chartered by the outward conference lines to New Zealand, and loading homewards on Blue Star's berth. On rare occasions an 'R' class ship was to be seen loading at a West Coast of the United States or Canadian port for Liverpool. The four remaining, bore 'S' names, although all were entirely different, trading on the New York service to Brazil and the River Plate via the West Indies.

On December 24, 1953 an interesting event occurred when the motorship *Rampart* (863 gross tons) departed from Liverpool on time-charter to the Lamport & Holt Line. It marked the inauguration of a direct service between the United Kingdom and the Paraguayan port of Asuncion by the company. The voyage, lasting seventy-seven days, was under the command of Captain W.C. Pargeter, of Ary Shipping Ltd., the *Rampart's* owners. Arriving at the Paraguayan capital on January 22, 1954, she was believed to be the first British ship ever to reach the port, no records being in existence of any other visit. After discharging general cargo, mainly consumer goods ranging from cosmetics, shoe polish and spirits, together with machinery and spares for Paraguayan export industries, she loaded tinned meats homewards, leaving Asuncion on January 30. So successful was this venture that more tonnage was chartered and a regular service commenced, subject to the levels of the Rivers Parana and Paraguay, which at that time were most difficult to navigate as there were no lights or buoys marking the channel. Eventually two ships were acquired specifically for this trade.

A further vessel was acquired for the New York service in 1954 when the *Sargeant* (3,843 gross tons) dating from 1945 arrived. It is interesting to note that Lamport & Holt registered her at Port of Spain, Trinidad for the eight years that she remained in the fleet and she was manned by a West Indian crew.

In 1954 the Vestey Group acquired a refrigerated ship *Mosdale* (3,022 gross tons) from Norwegian owners. She had traded for them since her completion by Burmeister and Wain, Copenhagen in 1939. At first she was placed under the ownership of Blue Star who had intended naming her *Trinidad Star*, but in the event called her *Albion Star*, but this was quickly changed and she became the *Balzac* for Lamport & Holt Line. She was to trade almost entirely with bananas from Santos to the United Kingdom and Continent, or on time-charter to Geest on their run from Dominica to Preston and occasionally Barry. In 1955 an almost identical vessel built a year earlier at the same shipyard as the *Barfleur* for French owners joined the fleet, becoming the *Boswell*. Both were good looking ships with their white painted hulls.

Blue Star were rapidly expanding their fleet engaged on the trade from Liverpool and Glasgow, where Lamport & Holt were their agents, to the North Pacific coast ports of North America and during 1954 and 1955 all five 'D' class ships were transferred to them, the *Delius* becoming the *Portland Star*; *Delane* – *Seattle Star*; *Defoe* – *Geelong Star*; *Debrett* – *Washington Star*; and the *Devis* – *Oakland Star*. In 1956 the *Debrett* and *Devis* reverted back to Lamport & Holt and their original names, followed in 1958 by the *Delius* and *Defoe*, but the *Delane* remained with Blue Star until sold out of the group in 1961.

During 1955 the service from New York as far South as Argentina and Uruguay was discontinued, and the remaining ships transferred back to the United Kingdom, or employed from New York to the West Indies, North Brazil and the Amazon. Close ties were established between them and the Booth Line ships so employed, and they began running in conjunction. At about this time an interest was taken in a service from Montreal to the West Indies and Georgetown. In the event the *Siddons* (3) and *Spenser* (3) were transferred back to the United Kingdom where they were renamed *Rubens* and *Roscoe* respectively, falling in with the 'R' class vessels on this route, although their size made them more useful trading to Brazilian ports.

Two ships arrived for the direct Asuncion service, the year old *Verdi* (571 gross tons) to Lamport & Holt in 1955 and the new *Virgil* (404 gross tons) on bareboat-charter from Panama Shipping, in 1956. At the same time the *Rossetti*, a sistership to the *Rubens* (ex-*Siddons*) arrived from Pickersgills at Sunderland.

A further 'R' class vessel appeared from Bartram and Sons Ltd., Sunderland in 1957; she was a sistership to the *Raphael*, and was named *Ronsard*. Initially she was registered at Hamilton, Bermuda, in the ownership of Salient Shipping Co. (Bermuda) Ltd., not transferring to the Liverpool register until 1960.

Two small motorships were built in 1959 for the New York service. They were particularly suitable for the Amazon trade since they were able to reach the Peruvian port of Iquitos. They were the *Siddons* of 1,282 gross tons from George Brown Ltd., Greenock, and the similar *Spenser* from Noderwerft Koser and Meyer, Hamburg.

During this year a 3,000 gross tons refrigerated ship was delivered from the yard of Brooke Marine Ltd., Lowestoft. Named *Constable* she was at the time the largest vessel delivered from this yard. A fast ship, with clipper-like lines, she was followed early the next year by a sister, the *Chatham* from A. Stephen and Sons Ltd., Linthouse. Both were used on a variety of trades, and were to be seen trading between Dominica and Preston and Barry on charter to Geest, but also trading to Trinidad, Santos and the East Coast of the United States from Dublin. Their much older consorts, *Balzac* and *Boswell* were renamed *Carroll* and *Crome* to fall into line with this 'C' class, but were soon transferred from Lamport & Holt within the group.

In 1961, a new motorship named *Sheridan* (3) of 1,535 gross tons arrived from T. van Duijvendijk's Scheepswerf N.V. Lekkerkerk, for the New York service, followed a year later by a sistership *Spenser* (5). The year 1967 saw the withdrawal of Lamport & Holt Line tonnage from New York when the two remaining ships were transferred to Booth. This connection, which had lasted for almost a hundred years, was carried on alone by the Booth Line until 1977, when they withdrew.

During 1974 the Vestey Group acquired premises at 30, James Street, Liverpool, from the Pacific Steam Navigation Company. This building was erected in 1892 as Oceanic House and was originally the headquarters of the White Star Line. The building was refurbished and renamed Albion House. This coincided with the formation of a new company, under the title 'Blue Star Ship Management Ltd.,' which took over responsibility for the ship husbandry of all the ships owned and/or operated by Lamport & Holt Line Ltd., the Booth Steamship Co. Ltd., and Blue Star Line Ltd., and was originally based at Liverpool, but almost a decade later was to be moved to Albion House, Leadenhall Street, London. During the earlier part of 1975 the managements of both Lamport & Holt and Booth Line moved to the new building at Albion House, Liverpool, thus the connection between Lamport & Holt and the Royal Liver Building, which had been its headquarters since 1912, came to an end.

By 1977 the Lamport & Holt fleet was down to four 'R' class vessels comprising the *Romney* (2) of 1952, *Roland* (2) of 1952, *Ronsard* of 1957 and the *Raeburn* (4) of 1957, all trading to Brazil and the River Plate.

Captain John Ivor Jones, DSO, DSC & Bar
Twice Mentioned in Despatches
Served with Lamport & Holt Line as Master 1958-1977

When I served with Lamport & Holt Line I knew of Captain Jones, but little else, not having served with him. I met him at Cardiff on board the *Raphael* in 1975 where he was kind enough to help with the history of the company, and gave me details of his career, not once mentioning his illustrious war service.

In 1936 he joined the Royal Naval Reserve, and at the outbreak of war in 1939 became a Sub-Lieutenant, where he pursued a most exciting career, taking part in the Norwegian campaign, thence to a Flower class corvette in the Mediterranean. As Lieutenant in command of HMS *Hyacinth*, he distinguished himself in the Greece/Crete campaign, both by his general efforts and by an act of gallantry when, as 'upside down Jones', he cleared his own propeller which had been fouled by the tow rope of a vessel he was attempting to tow clear from an occupied island while under enemy fire. For this he was awarded the DSC. Later, for capturing the Italian submarine *Perla*, one of the few submarines ever to be taken intact and delivering it in working order to the Port of Beirut, he collected a well deserved DSO. The Admiralty then promoted him to Lieutenant Commander in one of the elite Hunt class destroyers, operating in the Aegean. He later joined the Western Approaches anti-submarine frigates, remaining with them until the end of the war.

On reading Graeme Cubbin's book *Harrisons of Liverpool* (2003) I recognised references to him and his service with this other famous Liverpool company where he had held command from 1952 to 1955 and resigned following the stranding of the *Naturalist* off Anglesey on April 20, 1955, although the ship soon refloated and made port.

Whilst at this time 'his career (was) in ruins' you cannot keep a good man down. Captain Jones was a man of courage and integrity, and in 1956 he joined the Booth Line as Chief Officer on the service from New York to the West Indies and Amazon where he was highly thought of.

Mr. Lough, the General Manager of the Lamport & Holt Line was a hard but fair man, who could never be described as anybody's fool, for it was he who appointed Captain Jones as master with Lamport & Holt, a company in which he only ever served in that capacity. He served on Lamport & Holt's *Virgil* for seven months from July, 1958 on the United Kingdom to Paraguay direct service, followed by a single voyage on the *Memling* to Brazil and the River Plate, and a period as coastwise master. Thereafter he commanded the *Spenser* for fourteen months the last four after the ship transferred to Booth as the *Valiente*. This was on the trade from New York to the West Indies, North Brazil and Amazon as far up river as Iquitos in Peru. Then followed a single voyage on the *Ronsard*, until he was sent to the Netherlands to stand by the newbuilding *Spenser* which he took out to New York and commanded for twelve months, from May 4, 1962.

From September, 1963 he commanded the *Devis* (3), at 9,942 gross tons, by far Lamport & Holt's biggest cargo liner, for the six years that the company traded her until her sale at Belfast in June, 1969. A period coastwise was followed by two years as Master of the *Ronsard*. After another period coastwise he commanded the *Raeburn* for a single voyage to South Africa on time-charter. Thereafter he spent two more years with the *Ronsard* until January, 1975. When I met him he was master of the *Raphael* coastwise, and shortly after resumed his service with the *Ronsard* until his retirement in 1977. Alas he died a year later.

Captain Frank Martin
Served with Lamport & Holt Line 1955-1962
Master of 'Verdi' on three voyages on the Direct United Kingdom – Paraguay Service

I was appointed Master of the *Verdi* in April, 1961. The first voyage to Paraguay was cut short due to a drop in the River Paraguay. I was fortunate to be warned of the situation by the Dutch vessel *Nashira* which passed me on her way down river having turned back. A Danish vessel *Dita Smits* had been stranded and remained so for several weeks. *Nashira* and *Verdi* were both discharged at Santa Fe in Argentina. *Verdi* was at that time fitted with medium wave radio telephone and communication was always difficult after leaving the United Kingdom. Our agents in Asuncion had a transmitter but they could transmit only on short wave.

Verdi normally loaded general cargo in London or Liverpool for Asuncion. The passage to Montevideo averaged thirty-five days with a stop at Dakar for bunkers and provisions. I distinctly remember the first passage across the Bay of Biscay took eight days but she was an excellent sea boat.

The second voyage passed without incident and we managed to reach Asuncion without any delays. Homeward cargo was always corned beef. Two pilots were carried from Rosario to Asuncion and they did a marvellous job navigating in darkness without Radar and no shore lights or buoys to guide them. My only complaint about pilotage was when one Asuncion pilot took over for a stretch of about twenty miles and he was ninety years old and almost blind.

The third and last voyage for me on the *Verdi* was the one involving the towage of *Virgil*. *Virgil* called me on R/T as her main thrust bearing had been broken beyond repair. I took her in tow to Dakar, the towage lasting almost eight days, for which I received £800 salvage of which nearly half went in income tax. Due to the fact that the Master of the *Virgil* said they could not 'break' the cable for towage I had to tow with two mooring ropes tied end to end and ease the strain by paying out a little extra each day.

Towage Commenced at 05°13'N, 22°46'W at 1225 G.M.T. 3.4.1962

Arrived Dakar Roads 2115 G.M.T. 10.4.1962.

As in the case of the first voyage we could not get right up to Asuncion but we managed to get within about 50 miles. We tied up to trees on the river bank at a place called Pto Praia. We had to get fresh stores here and everything was 'live' so we had pigs and hens on deck for fresh meat until our return to Montevideo.

At the end of this voyage I left the sea to become a Pilot.

Although the *Verdi* commenced to tow the *Virgil* on April 3, the latter vessel actually broke down on March 28th, 1962.

Author's Note

In 1963 Lamport & Holt Line formed a wholly owned subsidiary – the Metric Line to operate coasters on charter for a service to the continent, normally Rotterdam, from Liverpool. In the event the *Verdi* and *Virgil* were sold, but chartered back for the purpose, and renamed *Kilo* and *Metre*. On the *Kilo's* first voyage on this service she was in distress in heavy weather when her cargo of sodium became wet and started to explode. The Tenby and Mumbles lifeboats which went to assist her were unable to catch her up in the bad weather. But eventually when she was beached off Swansea her crew were taken off by the Mumbles lifeboat. On refloating and repair she was returned to service.

The *Virgil*, with port lifeboat swung out under tow by the *Verdi*.   (*Capt. F. Martin*)

Two views (left and top of opposite page) of the *Verdi* moored to the River bank at Pto Praia, Argentina, where she unloaded her cargo into river craft.

(*Capt. F. Martin*)

FLEET LIST Part 9

Name & Period in Fleet	Gross tons	History
Siddons (3) 1952-1955 *Rubens* (2) 1955-1965 *Rossini* 1967-1970	4,459	Motorship. 1952 built by Wm. Pickersgill and Sons Ltd., Sunderland, as *Siddons* for Lamport & Holt Line Ltd.; 1955 renamed *Rubens*; 1965 bareboat chartered to Booth Steamship Co. Ltd., renamed *Bernard*; 1967 charter ended, renamed *Rossini*; 1970 to Booth Steamship Co. Ltd., renamed *Bernard*; 1973 to Sopac Bulk Carriers Co. Inc., Panama, renamed *Berwell Adventure*; 1974 to Booth Steamship Co. Ltd.; 1974 to Overseas Marine Corp., Panama; 1974 to Kelsey Bay Shipping Co. Ltd., Panama, renamed *Al Turab*; 1978 broken up at Gadani Beach.

The *Siddons* (3) operated out of New York to Brazil and the River Plate from 1952 to 1955, and was renamed *Rubens* (2) on transfer to the UK.

(*World Ship Photo Library*)

After trading as the *Rubens* for Lamport & Holt from 1955 to 1965 mainly on the Brazilian service, she spent a period with Booth Line finally returning to the company in 1967 as the *Rossini*.

(A. Duncan)

Name & Period in Fleet	Gross tons	History
Romney (2) 1952-1978	8,237	Steamship. 1952 built by Cammell Laird and Co. Ltd., Birkenhead, for Lamport & Holt Line Ltd.; 3.10.1978 arrived at Faslane for breaking up by Shipbreaking Industries Ltd.

The flagship *Romney* (2) at Las Palmas, Gran Canaria.

(Jose Verwaayen)

The turbine steamer *Romney* in the English Channel. *(Skyfotos Ltd.)*

Name & Period in Fleet	Gross tons	History

Raeburn (2)
1952-1958
Roland (2)
1977-1978

8,311

Motorship. 1952 built by Harland and Wolff Ltd., Belfast, for Lamport & Holt Line Ltd.; 1958 bareboat chartered to Blue Star Line Ltd., renamed *Colorado Star*; 1972 bareboat chartered to Austasia Line Ltd., Singapore, renamed *Mahsuri*; 1977 charter ended, renamed *Roland*; 5.10.1978 arrived at Faslane for breaking up by Shipbreaking Industries Ltd.

The *Raeburn* (2) traded as such from 1952 to 1958.
(*Skyfotos Ltd.*)

On return to Lamport & Holt in 1977 the *Raeburn* rejoined the fleet as the *Roland* (2).
(*A. Duncan*)

Raphael (2)
1953-1976

7,971

Motorship. 1953 built by Bartram and Sons Ltd., Sunderland, for Lamport & Holt Line Ltd.; 1976 to Carnation Shipping Co. Ltd., Limassol, renamed *Pola Rika*; 1977 to Allegro Marine Co. Ltd., Limassol; 1979 broken up at Gijon.

The *Raphael* (2) in the English Channel. (*Skyfotos Ltd.*)

125

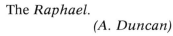

The *Raphael.*
(*A. Duncan*)

The *Raphael* at Vancouver on
March 14, 1959.
(*F.W. Hawks*)

Name & Period in Fleet	Gross tons	History
Dryden (4) 1953-1955 1963-1968	8,293	Motorship. 1939 built by Burmeister and Wain, Copenhagen, as *Columbia Star* for Blue Star Line Ltd.; 1950 to Lamport & Holt Line Ltd., bareboat chartered to Blue Star Line Ltd.; 1953 charter ended, renamed *Dryden*; 1955 bareboat chartered to Blue Star Line Ltd., renamed *Patagonia Star*; 1957 renamed *Columbia Star*; 1959 to Blue Star Line Ltd.; 1963 bareboat chartered to Lamport & Holt Line Ltd., renamed *Dryden*; 1966 to Lamport & Holt Line Ltd.; 10.11.1968 arrived at Kaohsiung for breaking up.

The *Dryden* (4).

Name & Period in Fleet	Gross tons	History
Sargent 1954-1962	3,843	Motorship. 1945 built by Walter Butler Shipbuilders Inc., Duluth., as *Frank J. Betrarca* for United States Maritime Commission; 1945 renamed *Roband Hitch*; 1946 to Panama Shipping Corp. Inc., bareboat chartered to Booth Steamship Co. Ltd., renamed *Jutahay*; 1954 to Lamport & Holt Line Ltd., Port of Registry – Port of Spain, Trinidad, renamed *Sargent*; 1962 to A. Halcoussis, Piraeus, renamed *Pamit*; 1966 to Bambero Cia. Nav. S.A., Monrovia, renamed *Bambero*; 3.3.1970 arrived at Castellon for breaking up by I.M. Varela Davalillo.
Balzac (2) 1954-1959 Carroll 1959-1960	3,022	Motorship. 1939 built by Burmeister and Wain, Copenhagen, as *Mosdale* for A/S Mosvold Shipping, Norway; 1954 to Blue Star Line Ltd., renamed *Albion Star*, (originally intended to name vessel *Trinidad Star*); 1954 to Lamport & Holt Line Ltd., renamed *Balzac*; 1959 renamed *Carroll*; 1960 to Blue Star Line Ltd., renamed *Norman Star*; 1960 bareboat chartered to Booth Steamship Co. Ltd., renamed *Basil*; 1964 to H. & D. Kyriakos, renamed *Eleni K*; 1966 to Helen Shipping Corporation (Panama) Ltd., Panama, renamed *Eleni Kyriakou*; 1970 renamed *Olga*; 1970 to Kreta Shipping Co. S.A., Piraeus, renamed *Georgios Markakis*; 1973 to Amarinthos Shipping Co. Ltd., Cyprus, renamed *Nikos*; 4.5.1973 arrived at Bilbao for breaking up.

Renamed *Carroll* in 1959 the reefer was previously the *Balzac* (2).

(World Ship Photo Library)

Name & Period in Fleet	Gross tons	History
Verdi (2) 1955-1963	571	Motorship. 1954 built by N.V. Scheepsbouwwerf v/h De Groot and Van Vliet, Slikkerveer, as *Hermes* for Brinkman, Kunst and Schokkenbroek, Netherlands; 1955 to Lamport & Holt Line Ltd., renamed *Verdi*; 1963 to N/V Scheeps-exploitatie Maatschappij 'Het Gein' and chartered for ten years to Metric Line Ltd. (Lamport & Holt Line Ltd.), renamed *Kilo*; 1974 to C. Englesos, Cyprus, renamed *Annet*; 1974 to Greek flag, renamed *Katopodis G*; 1977 to Katopodis Bros., Piraeus; 18.12.1977 inbound from Viareggio put ashore, leaking badly, in Derna Harbour, with hull cracks. Declared a constructive total loss.
Boswell (2) 1955-1960 *Crome* 1960	3,111	Motorship. 1938 built by Burmeister and Wain, Copenhagen, as *Barfleur* for Cie. Generale d'Armament Maritime, Paris; 1947 to Cie. Generale Transatlantique, Paris; 1955 to Blue Star Line Ltd.; 1955 to Lamport & Holt Line Ltd., renamed *Boswell*; 1960 renamed *Crome*; 1960 to Blue Star Line Ltd., renamed *Roman Star*; 1961 bareboat chartered to Booth Steamship Co. Ltd., renamed *Bede*; 1963 to Rahcassi Shipping Co. S.A., Greece, renamed *Victoria Elena*; 16.1.1967 caught fire while loading a cargo of cotton at Thessalonika, Greece; 19.1.1967 beached in a heavily damaged condition off Piraeus; declared a constructive total loss, refloated; 1967 broken up at La Spezia by Lotti S.p.A.
Virgil (2) 1956-1963	404	Motorship. 1956 built by Schiffsw A. Pahl, Hamburg as *Manstead*, but completed as *Virgil* for Panama Shipping Corp. Inc., bareboat chartered to Lamport & Holt Line Ltd.; 1963 to N/V Scheeps-exploitatie Maatschappij 'Het Gein' and chartered for ten years to Metric Line Ltd. (Lamport & Holt Line Ltd.), renamed *Metre*; 1974 to Ahmed Sayed Issa, Beirut, renamed *Amina*; 1977 to Hani Ahmed Majzoub and Shikri Khoury, Beirut; 1978 was laid up in need of repairs, with Lloyds rating suspended, but subsequently renewed; 1996 was still in service, no other details.

The Panama Shipping Corp motorship *Virgil* employed on the direct United Kingdom to Asuncion service.

(A. Duncan)

The 404 gross ton *Virgil* arriving at Montevideo from Asuncion in Spring, 1963 where she bunkered and reprovisioned before setting out on the long voyage home.

(P.M. Heaton)

Name & Period in Fleet	Gross tons	History
Rossetti (2) 1956-1963 1967-1970	4,693	Motorship. 1956 built by Wm. Pickersgill and Sons Ltd., Sunderland, for Lamport & Holt Line Ltd.; 1963 bareboat chartered to Booth Steamship Co. Ltd., renamed *Boniface*; 1967 charter ended, renamed *Rossetti*; 1970 to Booth Steamship Co. Ltd., renamed *Boniface*; 1974 to Hydra Navigation Co. Ltd., Piraeus, renamed *Amaryllis*; 1978 to Imerama S.A., Piraeus, renamed *Zefyros*; 1979 broken up at Kaohsiung.

The *Rossetti* (2).
(Skyfotos Ltd.)

Name & Period in Fleet	Gross tons	History

Ronsard
1957-1980

7,840

Motorship. 1957 built by Bartram and Sons Ltd., Sunderland, for Salient Shipping Co. (Bermuda) Ltd., Hamilton, and bareboat chartered to Lamport & Holt Line Ltd.; 1960 to Lamport & Holt Line Ltd.; 1980 to Obestein Inc., Panama, renamed *Obestein*; 1981 broken up at Kaohsiung.

The *Ronsard* was bareboat chartered from Salient Shipping Co. (Bermuda) Ltd, not transferring to the Liverpool register until 1960.   (A. Duncan)

The *Ronsard* in the English Channel.   (Skyfotos Ltd.)

Murillo (3)
1957-1961

7,197

Steamship. 1944 built by Lithgows Ltd., Port Glasgow, as *Empire Talisman* for Ministry of War Transport (Blue Star Line Ltd.); 1946 bareboat chartered to Blue Star Line Ltd.; 1949 to Blue Star Line Ltd., renamed *Tacoma Star*; 1957 to Lamport & Holt Line Ltd., renamed *Murillo*; 1957 to Blue Star Line Ltd., and bareboat chartered to Lamport & Holt Line Ltd.; 16.3.1961 arrived at Vigo for breaking up.

The *Murillo* (3) transferred from Blue Star Line in 1957.
(A. Duncan)

Name & Period in Fleet	Gross tons	History
Millais (3) 1957-1960	7,053	Steamship. 1944 built by Short Bros, Ltd., Sunderland, as *Empire Pendennis* for Ministry of War Transport (Ellerman Lines); 1946 to Cunard White Star Line Ltd., Liverpool, renamed *Vasconia*; 1949 to Cunard Steamship Co. Ltd., Liverpool; 1951 to Blue Star Line Ltd., renamed *Fresno Star*; 1957 to Lamport & Holt Line Ltd., renamed *Millais*; 1957 to Blue Star Line Ltd., and bareboat chartered to Lamport & Holt Line Ltd.; 1960 to Grosvenor Shipping Co. Ltd., (Moller's Ltd.,) Hong Kong, renamed *Grosvenor Navigator*; 9.9.1966 arrived Kaohsiung for breaking up.

The *Millais* (3) also came from Blue Star in 1957.
(A. Duncan)

Sallust (3) 1958-1959	3,381	Motorship. 1945 built by Leatham D. Smith Shipbuilding Corp., Sturgeon Bay, Wisconsin, for United States Maritime Commission, launched as *Tulare*, but completed as *Coastal Challenger*; 1946 to Panama Shipping Corp. Inc., bareboat chartered to Booth Steamship Co. Ltd., renamed *Pachitea*; 1954 to Booth Steamship Co. Ltd., renamed *Dunstan*; 1958 to Lamport & Holt Line Ltd., renamed *Sallust*; 1959 to Austasia Line Ltd., Singapore, renamed *Malacca*; 1962 to Kie Hock Shipping (Hong Kong) Ltd., Hong Kong, renamed *Tong Hong*; 25.10.1967 left Kawasaki for Singapore on a voyage to Colombo with a cargo of Ammonium sulphate, and lost without trace.
Siddons (4) 1959-1962	1,282	Motorship. 1959 built by Geo. Brown Ltd., Greenock; laid down for Blue Star Line Ltd., but completed as *Siddons* for Lamport & Holt Line Ltd.; 1962 bareboat chartered to Booth Steamship Co. Ltd., renamed *Veras*; 1966 lengthened at Hamburg, gross tonnage increased to 1,616; 1973 to Ghania Cia. Nav. S.A., Panama, renamed *Kydonia*; 1976 to Fayrouz Cia. Nav. S.A., Panama, renamed *Fayrouz*; 4.10.1978 damaged by fire at Piraeus while undertaking repairs; damage so severe that broken up at Perama.

Name & Period in Fleet	Gross tons	History
Spenser (4) 1959-1961	1,312	Motorship. 1959 built by Norderwerft Koser and Meyer, Hamburg, for Lamport & Holt Line Ltd.; 1961 to Panama Shipping Corp. Inc. bareboat chartered to Booth Steamship Co. Ltd., renamed *Valiente*; 1964 lengthened, gross tonnage increased to 1,609; 1969 renamed *Veloz*; 1973 to Compania National de Nav. S.A. (Navenal), Bogota, renamed *Tanambi*; 23.8.1979 grounded in the Panama Canal, while on passage from Buena Ventura to Guanta, refloated; 2.12.1982 arrived at Cartagena, Colombia, for breaking up.
Constable 1959-1962	3,099	Motorship. 1959 built by Brooke Marine Ltd., Lowestoft, for Lamport & Holt Line Ltd.; 1962 to Blue Star Line Ltd., renamed *Santos Star*; 1964 lengthened by Harland and Wolff Ltd., Belfast, gross tonnage increased to 3,775; 1966 to Calmedia S.p.A. di Nav., Cagliari, renamed *Calagaribaldi*; 1981 to Nourfo Compania Naviera S.A., Panama, renamed *Gafredo*; 29.4.1984 arrived at Barcelona for breaking up.

The reefer *Constable* built at Lowestoft in 1959. *(Skyfotos Ltd.)*

Name & Period in Fleet	Gross tons	History
Chatham (2) 1960-1962	3,005	Motorship. 1960 built by A. Stephen and Sons Ltd., Linthouse, for Lamport & Holt Line Ltd.; 1962 to Blue Star Line Ltd., renamed *Mendoza Star*; 1963 lengthened at Hoboken, Belgium, gross tonnage increased to 3,666; 1967 to Calmedia S.p.A. di Nav., Cagliari, renamed *Calavittoria*; 1979 to Laguna Shipping Co. (Laskaridis Shipping Co. Ltd.), Piraeus, renamed *Frio Aegean*; 1981 to Tobermory Shipping Co. S.A., (Laskaridis Shipping Co. Ltd.), Panama; 26.3.1984 arrived at Gadani Beach for breaking up.

The clipper like *Chatham* (2) arrived in the fleet in 1960.
(Skyfotos Ltd.)

The *Chatham* on passage London to Port of Spain in September, 1961. Looking forward in Hurricane 'Debbie'. *(P.M. Heaton)*

Looking aft in Hurricane 'Debbie'. *(P.M. Heaton)*

The *Chatham* on passage Buenos Aires to Hamburg in February, 1962. Three deck views.

(*P.M. Heaton*)

Sheridan (3)
1961-1967   1,535

Motorship. 1961 built by T. van Duijvendijk Scheepswerf N.V., Lekkerkerk, for Booth Steamship Co. Ltd., and bareboat chartered to Lamport & Holt Line Ltd.; 1964 to Lamport and Holt Line Ltd; 1964 lengthened by Smith's Dock Co. Ltd., North Shields, gross tonnage increased to 1,849; 1967 bareboat chartered to Booth Steamship Co. Ltd., renamed *Cyril*; 1973 to Panama Shipping Corp. Inc., bareboat chartered to Booth Steamship Co. Ltd.; 1978 to Altis Shipping Co. S.A., Piraeus, renamed *Angie*; 1979 to Ocean Breeze Cia. Nav. S.A., Piraeus; 1980 to Aegaeus Maritime Co. S.A., Piraeus, renamed *Amalia*; 1981 to Wes Line Co. Ltd., Panama, renamed *West Point*; 1985 to Perkapalan Sri Tomah Sendirian Berhad, Malaysia, renamed *Tumoh Saty*; 6.1994 broken up at Singapore by Natsteel Shipbreakers Pte. Ltd.

The *Sheridan* (3) built in 1961 for the New York, West Indies, Amazon service. *(A. Duncan)*

Name & Period in Fleet	Gross tons	History
Spenser (5) 1962-1967	1,549	Motorship. 1962 built by T. van Duijvendijk Scheepswerf N.V., Lekkerkerk, for Booth Steamship Co. Ltd., bareboat chartered to Lamport & Holt Line Ltd.; 1964 lengthened at Smith's Dock Co. Ltd., North Shields, gross tonnage increased to 1,869; 1964 to Lamport & Holt Line Ltd.; 1967 bareboat chartered to Booth Steamship Co. Ltd. renamed *Cuthbert*; 1973 to Panama Shipping Corp. Inc., bareboat chartered to Booth Steamship Co. Ltd.; 1977 to Associated Levant Lines S.A.L., Beirut, renamed *Barouk*; 1982 to Naviera An Hing S. de R.L., Vanuata, renamed *An Hing*; 1982 to Guangzhou Ocean Shipping Co., Guangzhou; 1987 to Hai Win Co., Panama, renamed *Hai Win*; 1.12.1988 classification suspended, repairs needed; 5.1996 believed lying abandoned near Saigon, no other details.
Rossetti (3) 1963-1964	5,664	Motorship. 1963 Watts, Watts & Co's *Woodford* time-chartered by Lamport & Holt Line Ltd and renamed *Rossetti*; 1964 at charter end reverted to *Woodford*.

Watts, Watts M.V. *Woodford* on charter to Lamport & Holt Line 1963/64. She was renamed *Rossetti*.
(A. Duncan)

| *Raeburn* (3) 1963-1964 | 5,664 | Motorship. 1963 Watts, Watts & Co's *Wanstead* time-chartered by Lamport & Holt Line Ltd and renamed *Raeburn*; 1964 at charter end reverted to *Wanstead*. |

Watts, Watts *Wanstead* trading as the *Raeburn* on time-charter to Lamport & Holt 1963/64.
(A. Duncan)

Rossetti (4) 1964	9,221	Motorship. 1964 Watts, Watts & Co's *Weybridge* time-chartered by Lamport & Holt Line Ltd and renamed *Rossetti*; 1964 at charter end reverted to *Weybridge*.
Rubens (3) 1966-1973	4,472	Steamship. 1951 built by Wm. Pickersgill and Sons Ltd., Sunderland, as *Crispin* for Booth Steamship Co. Ltd.; 1954 to Austasia Line Ltd., Singapore, renamed *Mandowi*; 1966 to Booth Steamship Co. Ltd., renamed *Dunstan*; 1966 bareboat chartered to Lamport & Holt Line Ltd., renamed *Rubens*; 1973 to George Kaiogeras, Piraeus, renamed *Irini K*; 24.4.1974 arrived at Istanbul for breaking up.

The *Rubens* (3) was fifteen years old when acquired in 1966.   *(Skyfotos Ltd.)*

The *Rubens.*
(A. Duncan)

Name & Period in Fleet	Gross tons	History

Renoir
1967-1971

4,300

Motorship. 1953 built by Wm. Pickersgill and Sons Ltd., Sunderland; laid down as *Clement* for Booth Steamship Co. Ltd.; launched as *Malay Star* for Blue Star Line Ltd., and completed as *Malay* for Austasia Line Ltd., Singapore; 1964 renamed *Mahsuri*; 1966 to Booth Steamship Co. Ltd., renamed *Benedict*; 1967 bareboat chartered to Lamport & Holt Line Ltd., renamed *Renoir*; 1971 to Starlight Steamship Co. S.A., Panama, renamed *Diamond Star*; 1973 broken up at Suao, Taiwan.

The *Renoir* carrying the Austasia Line's funnel colours. *(A. Duncan)*

Roland (1)
1968-1975

7,344

Steamship. 1950 built by A. Stephen and Sons Ltd., Linthouse, laid down as *Bolton Castle* for Lancashire Shipping Co. Ltd., (Mollers Trust Ltd.) Hong Kong; to Blue Star Line Ltd while on stocks and completed as *Dunedin Star*; 1968 to Lamport & Holt Line Ltd., renamed *Roland*; 1975 to Pallas Maritime Co., Limassol, renamed *Jessica*; 1975 to Alligator Shipping Co., Limassol, who bought the ship to resell for scrap; 17.7.1976 arrived at Karachi, where she passed a special survey, and her owners decided to trade vessel; 10.6.1978 arrived at Gadani Beach for breaking up.

Formerly the *Dunedin Star* the *Roland* (1) served Lamport & Holt from 1968 to 1975.

(A. Duncan)

Name & Period in Fleet	Gross tons	History
Raeburn (4) 1972-1979	6,274	Motorship. 1957 built by Caledon Shipbuilding & Engineering Co. Ltd., Dundee, as *Canadian Star* for Blue Star Line Ltd.; 1972 bareboat chartered to Lamport & Holt Line Ltd., renamed *Raeburn*; 1975 to Lamport & Holt Line Ltd.; 1979 to Vertigo Shipping Co. Ltd., Panama, renamed *Braeburn*; 1979 to Ahmed Shipping Lines, Panama; 20.4.1979 arrived at Kaohsiung for breaking up.

The *Raeburn* (4) was formerly Blue Star Line's *Canadian Star*.　　　　　　　　　　　(A. Duncan)

12. CONTAINERISATION – TRIUMPH AND TRAGEDY

There has been a dramatic change in South America's trade with Europe since the 1950s, brought about by the growth of industrial Brazil and the countries of the River Plate region. This dynamic development had produced spectacular sky-scraping cities, expanding industries, and exploitation of mineral and agricultural resources on a hitherto undreamed of scale. The South American countries no longer rely solely on their pastoral and agricultural resources, and acting as markets for imported manufactured goods. These nations themselves now export a considerable range of manufactured and processed goods. Cargo from Brazil these days includes footwear, copper tubes, textiles and other finished products. There is still a large movement of coffee, cotton, cocoa and timber. But there is an increasing tendency for these to be shipped in semi-manufactured or processed form; soluble coffee, cocoa, butter, timber products such as parquet, door lippings, plywoods, and a wide range of veneers and hardwoods. Exports from Argentina include motor vehicle parts and iron and steel products as well as canned meat and fruit, wine as well as wool and animal foodstuffs in bulk, in processed forms such as pellets, extracts and meals. Ships take to Brazil and River Plate, sophisticated machinery, machine tools, and other equipment for the new factories. Sometimes whole factories or blast furnaces are carried. As part of this industrialisation and development there has been a considerable expansion of their national shipping lines, and these carry a considerable share of the trade.[1]

Lamport & Holt Line, by the mid-1970s had a fine, but nevertheless elderly fleet of four 'R' class vessels. Indications from shippers were that a break bulk vessel with some container capacity would be required in the South American East Coast trades for a number of years to come, and therefore the management set about studying proposals for the best possible replacements for the fleet. The result was to see the ordering in June, 1976 of four of the successful SD14 cargo ships from the yard of Austin and Pickersgill Ltd., Sunderland. The vessels, built to the latest fourth series design, were to be 15,265 tonnes deadweight and equipped to carry 118-20 ft containers in the holds, on the hatch covers and on the upper deck. Four of the five holds were fitted with a tween deck whilst the other had provision for the carriage of edible oil. Cargo handling equipment comprising one 26 tonne and three 22 tonne 'Velle' derricks serving the forward hatches and two 5 tonne derricks at No. 5 hatch.

The four ships were duly completed in 1979 and 1980, and entered service as the 'B' class, named *Bronte* (3), *Browning* (3), *Boswell* (3) and *Belloc*. The older 'R' class vessels were disposed of, the *Romney* (2) being broken up at Faslane in 1978, while the *Ronsard* and *Raeburn* (4) were sold for further trading. The new vessels joined the Joint British Line's service to the East Coast of South America, comprising Blue Star Line, Houlder Bros., Lamport & Holt Line and Royal Mail Lines, trading as BHLR, where their appearance was most welcome. However their entry into service did regrettably mark the end of the passenger service as, unlike the 'R' class before them, none had any passenger accommodation.

During 1981 the BHLR service was extended to offer a fully containerised sailing from the United Kingdom to the East Coast of South America, using two time-chartered vessels of moderate size, and gradually the demand for container capacity increased. As a result of the Falklands War a larger vessel with greater container capacity was required to transport construction equipment and materials for the new airport, and as a result the four 'B' class ships were gradually disposed of to other owners, and in 1983 the 12,214 gross ton motorship *Ruddbank* was acquired from the Bank Line and renamed *Romney* (3). She saw service outwards to the Falklands and loaded homewards at Montevideo and Brazil, and continued in service until the completion of the project in the South Atlantic. Thereafter she was disposed of.

Meanwhile it was decided to rationalise the BHLR service by using larger vessels and renaming the service as the Brisa Line (British South America Lines). At the same time the management of the joint service was integrated into one central office at 46/50, Gun Street, London, which marked its incorporation into a consortium of European and South American Lines, operating nine similar container ships within a common schedule. A conventional/break bulk service was also offered from South America to Liverpool, Belfast and Dublin.

As a result of these developments Lamport & Holt Line and Blue Star Line decided to convert an existing group vessel to make her suitable for this service. As a result the *New Zealand Star*, which had been built in 1979 by Smith's Dock Co. Ltd., Middlesbrough, for Blue Star Line's New Zealand – Australia – The Gulf – Karachi – Bombay – Cochin – Colombo – Singapore – New Zealand service, was selected. She was sent to the Jurong Shipyard at Singapore in January, 1986 for lengthening and refurbishment. This increased her container capacity from 721 to 1,143 and her gross tonnage from 17,082 to 22,635, effectively increasing her capacity by 84 per cent. At the same time her accommodation was refurbished, and facilities for twelve passengers provided in five double and two single cabins with their own private facilities.

1 – Journal of Commerce – 1975

On completion of the work, the vessel was repainted in Lamport & Holt Line colours, and renamed *Churchill* after that most respected British Statesman, prolific author and renowned artist. She sailed from Singapore for Montevideo where in April, 1986 she joined the Brisa Line service Northbound. Her schedule took in the following ports: Tilbury – Hamburg – Bremen – Antwerp – Salvador – Santos – Montevideo – later Buenos Aires – Rio Grande do Sul – Sao Francisco do Sul – Santos – Salvador – Rotterdam – Tilbury (with an occasional call at Recife).

On May 12, 1986 the *Churchill* was welcomed at Tilbury Dock where Lady Soames, daughter of the late Sir Winston Churchill, named the vessel, which was the largest ever to carry the company's colours.

Alas nothing lasts forever. The takeover at the end of 1990 of the Furness Withy Group, owners of Royal Mail Lines and Houlder Bros., by the German Oetker family, better known as Hamburg Sud and Columbus Line, led to changes which culminated in their decision to withdraw from the Brisa Line partnership, which ceased trading as a shipping line on June 30, 1991. New arrangements came into effect and the Vestey Group decided to operate on the South American trade under the 'Blue Star Line' banner. The Lamport & Holt conference rights were amalgamated into Blue Star and the *Churchill* was renamed *Argentina Star*.

Thus after 146 years the Lamport & Holt Line disappeared – my sadness is complete.

FLEET LIST Part 10

Name & Period in Fleet	Gross tons	History
Bronte (3) 1979-1983	9,324	Motorship. 1979 built by Austin & Pickersgill Ltd., Sunderland, for Lamport & Holt Line Ltd.; 1983 to China Ocean Shipping, Canton, renamed *An Dong Jiang*; 1990 to Fortunate Star Marine Ltd., Valletta (China Ocean Shipping), renamed *Safe Star*; 2001 Flag and port of registry deleted from Lloyd's Register; believed renamed *An Dong Jiang*; Understood to be still trading.

The *Bronte* (3) on trials early in 1979.
Turners (Photography) Ltd.

The *Bronte. (A. Duncan)*

Name & Period in Fleet	Gross tons	History
Browning (3) 1979-1983	9,324	Motorship. 1979 built by Austin & Pickersgill Ltd., Sunderland, for Lamport & Holt Line Ltd.; 1983 to China Ocean Shipping, Canton renamed *An Fu Jiang*; 1990 to Fortunate Star Marine Ltd., Valletta, (China Ocean Shipping), renamed *Fortunate Star*; 2000 to Ocean Join Shipping Inc., Panama, renamed *Ocean Join*; 2004 still trading.

The SD14 *Browning*.
(A. Duncan)

An impressive view of the *Browning* in the English Channel.　　　　(*Skyfotos Ltd.*)

Name & Period in Fleet	Gross tons	History
Boswell (3) 1979-1983	9,324	Motorship. 1979 built by Austin & Pickersgill Ltd., Sunderland, for Lamport & Holt Line Ltd.; 1983 to Chinese-Tanzanian Joint Shipping Co., Canton, renamed *Shun Yi*; 2002 Reported classification withdrawn; reported renamed *XI Run*; status unknown.

Boswell.   (A. Duncan)

The *Boswell* (3).   (*Skyfotos Ltd.*)

Name & Period in Fleet	Gross tons	History
Belloc 1980-1981	9,324	Motorship. 1980 built by Austin & Pickersgill Ltd., Sunderland, for Lamport & Holt Line., 1981 to Montenegro Overseas Navigation Ltd. Inc., Panama, renamed *Piva*; 1992 to Bar Overseas Shipping Ltd., Valletta, renamed *Rio B*; owners later recorded as Domino Shipping Co. Ltd. (Prekookeanska Plovidba, Bar), renamed *Pangani*; 2000 to Yong Shun Shipping Private Ltd Singapore; 2004 still trading.

Launch of the *Belloc* at Austin & Pickersgill's yard at Sunderland on May 10, 1979. She was the last ship built for the Lamport & Holt Line.

Authors Note

Having served with the Lamport & Holt Line Ltd in the early 1960s, and living in South Wales, I rarely saw one of their ships.

However, I followed their fortunes over the years, and was pleased to note that four SD14 cargo ships had been ordered from Austin & Pickersgill Ltd., at Sunderland. Through the kindness of John Lingwood, who served with the builders, on May 10, 1979, I was able to attend the launching of the final Lamport & Holt SD14, the *Belloc*, and saw the earlier vessel *Boswell* fitting out. It was a wonderful occasion, and little did I know that I was witnessing the launch of the last ever vessel built to the company's own order.

It was the last time I ever saw a Lamport & Holt Line ship.

The *Belloc* in the English Channel. (*Skyfotos Ltd.*)

Name & Period in Fleet	Gross tons	History
Romney (3) 1983-1986	12,214	Motorship. 1979 built by Sunderland Shipbuilders Ltd., Sunderland, as *Ruddbank* for the Bank Line Ltd. (Andrew Weir & Co. Ltd.), London; 1983 to Lamport & Holt Line Ltd., renamed *Romney*; 1986 to Highvale Ltd. (Lion Shipping Co.), Hong Kong, renamed *Lairg*; 1989 renamed *Napier Star* 1991 to Tamapatcharee Shipping Co. Ltd., Hong Kong, renamed *Tamapatcharee*; 1996 to South Asia Shipping Ltd., Hong Kong, renamed *Lady Rebecca*; 1998 –

The *Romney* (3) acquired in 1983 was formerly Bank Line's *Ruddbank*.   (*Paul Boot*)

The *Romney* (3).   *(Paul Boot)*

Name & Period in Fleet	Gross tons	History
Churchill 1986-1991	22,635	Motorship. 1979 built by Smiths Dock Co. Ltd., Middlesbrough, as *New Zealand Star* for Blue Star Line Ltd.; Original gross tonnage was 17,082; 1986 lengthened and new wider midship section inserted at Singapore, to Lamport & Holt Line Ltd., renamed *Churchill*; 1991 to Blue Star Line Ltd., renamed *Argentina Star*; 1998 –

Built in 1979 as the *New Zealand Star*, the *Churchill* was lengthened at Singapore for the Europe to East Coast of South American Container Service.

(FotoFlite)

The *Churchill* with a capacity of 1,143 containers, was one of the nine such ships operating in a Consortium between Europe and the East coast of South America. *(FotoFlite)*

The *Churchill* entered Lamport & Holt Line service in April, 1986 when she commenced loading at Montevideo for Europe. She is seen in the English Channel in May, 1986 outward bound for Brazil. *(FotoFlite)*

No longer serving Liverpool, the last Lamport & Holt ship *Churchill* was registered at London. *(FotoFlite)*

Author's Note
Following the Blue Star Lines acquisition of Lamport & Holt Line, various transfers took place between the Vestey Group constituent companies, and this has been shown in the fleet list. However, the 'dates in fleet' have always been given as those where the vessel has been operated by Lamport & Holt. There were a number of Blue Star Line ships which were never operated by Lamport & Holt, but for varying periods were registered in their ownership. They have not been included in the fleet list, but for the sake of clarity are listed hereunder.

Name	Year Built	Gross tonnage	Period Owned
Rhodesia Star	1943	8,642	1949-1959
New Zealand Star	1935	10,746	1950-1953
Brisbane Star	1937	11,076	1950-1959
Timaru Star	1945	7,930	1950-1959
Napier Star	1942	7,166	1950-1953
Empire Star	1946	11,085	1950-1971
Scottish Star	1950	10,174	1964-1970
Queensland Star	1957	9,920	1964-1965
Rockhampton Star	1957	10,619	1964-1965
Adelaide Star	1950	12,964	1964-1965
Ulster Star	1959	10,413	1964-1965
Fremantle Star	1960	8,403	1964-1965

MARINE AND WAR LOSSES

Date	Vessel	Type	Details
1855	*Junior*	Barque	Wrecked – no other details.
2.1856	*Simoda*	Ship	Wrecked in the Dardanelles, whilst on charter to the British Government as a Crimea War transport.
1857	*Cathaya*	Barque	Lost at sea – no other details.
1865	*Grasmere*	Ship	Lost at sea – no other details.
1865	*Coniston*	Barque	Wrecked – no other details.
1868	*Breeze*	Snow	Went missing.
21.1.1873	*Talisman*	Steamship	Foundered North West of the Burlings, Portugal.
24.11.1873	*Flamsteed* (1)	Steamship	Outward bound, lost in collision with HMS *Bellerphon*.
28.2.1875	*Maraldi*	Steamship	Wrecked near Pernambuco, while on passage Montevideo to Antwerp.
9.4.1881	*Newton* (1)	Steamship	Wrecked off Madeira, while on passage Rio de Janeiro to London.
13.5.1882	*Pliny*	Steamship	Wrecked off New Jersey, while on passage Rio de Janeiro to New York.
26.2.1883	*Copernicus* (1)	Steamship	Wrecked at Porto de Pedras, Brazil, while on passage Liverpool to Bahia.
1889	*Como*	Steamship	Wrecked – no other details.
1891	*No. 3*	Lighter	Wrecked – no other details.
29.2.1892	*Plato*	Steamship	Main shaft broke, 160 miles South West of the Scilly Isles, while on passage Liverpool to Brazil; foundered the next day (1.3.1892)
23.3.1893	*Flamsteed* (2)	Steamship	Wrecked by grounding near Imperial River, Chile, while on passage Antwerp to Valparaiso; broken up where she lay.
1893	*Brenda*	Steamship	Wrecked – no other details.
22.6.1895	*Bessel*	Steamship	Lost in collision with the Wilson Line's *Hero* in the English Channel, West of the Royal Sovereign Lightship, while on passage London to Brazil.
28.9.1895	*Dalton*	Steamship	Wrecked on the Isle of Islay, while on passage New York to the Clyde.
16.10.1895	*Copernicus* (3)	Steamship	Went missing while on passage, Sandy Point, New York to Valparaiso.

Date	Vessel	Type	Details
17.10.1896	*Chantrey*	Steamship	Wrecked near Valparaiso, while on passage Quayaquil to Buenos Aires.
9.3.1900	*Cuvier*	Steamship	Lost in collision with the steamer *Dovre* off the East Goodwin Lightship while on passage Antwerp to Brazil; 26 lives were lost, only three survivors.
1.10.1900	*Biela* (1)	Steamship	Lost in collision with the steamer *Eagle Point* off Nantucket, while on passage New York to Liverpool.
1.8.1902	*Wordsworth*	Steamship	Wrecked near Bahia, while on passage from New York.
31.1.1903	*Maskelyne*	Steamship	Foundered in the Atlantic in position 41°.35'N, 34°.40'W, while on passage New Orleans to Antwerp.
16.10.1908	*Velasquez*	Steamship	Wrecked at Sao Sebastiano, near Santos, while on a voyage Buenos Aires to New York.
15.6.1911	*Milton*	Steamship	Wrecked off Portugal near Cabo Espichel, while on passage London to Santos.
23.1.1912	*Calderon* (2)	Steamship	Broke in two after a collision with the steamer *Musketeer* in the Crosby Channel, River Mersey; total loss.
16.1.1913	*Veronese*	Steamship	Wrecked near Leixoes, Portugal, while on a voyage from Liverpool to the River Plate, with the loss of 27 lives.
8.10.1914	*Cervantes* (2)	Steamship	Sunk by the German cruiser *Karlsruhe* 100 miles South West of St. Paul's Rock.
26.10.1914	*Vandyck* (2)	Steamship	Sunk by the German cruiser *Karlsruhe* 690 miles West of St. Paul's Rock.
9.2.1916	*Horace*	Steamship	Sunk by the German raider *Moewe* 600 miles North East of Pernambuco.
2.12.1916	*Voltaire* (1)	Steamship	Sunk by the German raider *Moewe* 650 miles West of Fastnet.
17.12.1916	*Pascal* (2)	Steamship	Torpedoed and sunk by *U70* seven miles off the Casquets, while on passage Halifax to Cherbourg; 2 crew killed, master taken prisoner.
28.4.1917	*Terence*	Steamship	Torpedoed and sunk by *U81* 150 miles North West of Fastnet, while on passage Buenos Aires to Liverpool; one crew member killed.
30.4.1917	*Colbert*	Steamship	Torpedoed and sunk in the Mediterranean.

Date	Vessel	Type	Details
22.8.1917	*Verdi* (1)	Steamship	Torpedoed and sunk by *U53* 115 miles North West of Eagle Island, while on passage New York to Liverpool; 6 lives lost.
26.8.1917	*Titian*	Steamship	Torpedoed and sunk by *U14* South East of Malta, while on passage London to Alexandria.
3.10.1917	*Memling* (2)	Steamship	Torpedoed off Brest; so badly damaged, with a broken back and damaged engine, although she made port was declared a constructive total loss and broken up.
6.1.1918	*Spenser* (2)	Steamship	Torpedoed and sunk by *U61* off Bardsey Island, Irish Sea.
12.11.1928	*Vestris*	Steamship	Foundered off Virginia Cape, while on a voyage from New York to Buenos Aires with the loss of 112 lives.
1.5.1938	*Nasmyth* (2)	Steamship	Grounded at Tanife Point, Grand Canaria; Refloated, towed to the UK where declared a constructive total loss and broken up.
23.8.1939	*Linnell*	Motorship	Stranded at Alexandria, refloated, but on return to UK was broken up.
27.10.1939	*Bronte* (1)	Steamship	Torpedoed and damaged by *U34* South West of Ireland in convoy while on passage Liverpool to Rosario via Halifax; efforts to tow her in failed and on 30.10.1939 she was sunk by escorts.
10.6.1940	*Vandyck* (3)	Steamship	Whilst serving as HMS *Vandyck* was bombed and sunk off Narvik with the loss of 7 crew; the remainder captured and taken prisoner.
7.7.1940	*Delambre* (2)	Steamship	Captured and sunk by the German raider *Thor* North West of Ascension Island.
15.10.1940	*Bonheur*	Steamship	Torpedoed and sunk by *U138* North West of Cape Wrath, while on passage Liverpool to Rosario.
26.2.1941	*Swinburne*	Steamship	Bombed and damaged by aircraft West of Ireland; sunk by escort.
9.4.1941	*Voltaire* (2)	Steamship	Whilst serving as HMS *Voltaire* sunk by the German raider *Thor* with the loss of 75 lives.
30.4.1941	*Lassell* (2)	Motorship	Torpedoed and sunk by *U107* while on passage UK to Rio de Janeiro; 2 crew killed at that time. Of the two lifeboats one was picked up by Elder Dempster's *Egba* and survivors landed at Freetown; the other was picked up by Ben Line's *Benvrachie* which herself was torpedoed and sunk with the further loss of 15 of *Lassell's* crew.

Date	Vessel	Type	Details
20.5.1941	*Cockaponset*	Steamship	Managed by the company for the Ministry of War Transport; Torpedoed and sunk by *U111* South of Cape Farewell, while on passage in convoy Houston-Holyhead-Cardiff.
8.6.1941	*Phidias* (2)	Steamship	Shelled and sunk by *U46* North of the Azores, while on passage the Clyde to Cape Town; 8 crew lost.
22.6.1941	*Balzac* (1)	Steamship	Shelled and sunk by the German raider *Atlantis* North East of Para, while on a voyage Rangoon to Liverpool with the loss of 4 crew; The single gun on the *Balzac* had returned such accurate fire that the raider used a considerable amount of ammunition, thereafter being short and cutting down the period of her cruise. It didn't save the *Balzac*, but undoubtedly saved other Allied vessels.
14.2.1942	*Biela* (2)	Steamship	Torpedoed and sunk by *U98* East of Cape Race while on passage Liverpool to Buenos Aires with the loss of all 56 on board.
24.6.1942	*Willimantic*	Steamship	Managed by the company for the Ministry of War Transport; Shelled and sunk by *U156* in mid-Atlantic, while on passage Cape Town to Charleston, Virginia, with the loss of a number of crew.
23.9.1942	*Bruyere*	Steamship	Torpedoed and sunk by *U125* South West of Freetown, while on passage Buenos Aires to Liverpool.
24.9.1942	*Defoe* (1)	Motorship	While on passage Manchester to Madagascar, she was abandoned after an explosion and fire on board West of Rockall. Carrying Aircraft varnish and drums of liquid chlorine in her No. 1 hold, her bow was blown off up to the fore mast. Subsequently sank – not directly due to enemy action.
29.10.1942	*Laplace* (2)	Steamship	Torpedoed and sunk by *U159* South of Cape Agulhas, Cape of Good Hope, while on passage Port Said – Lourenco Marques – Buenos Aires.
12.11.1942	*Browning* (1)	Steamship	Torpedoed and sunk by *U595* off Oran; one crew member lost.
1.7.1943	*Empire Ibex*	Steamship	Managed by the company for the Ministry of War Transport; damaged in collision with an aircraft carrier; 2.7.1943 abandoned; 3.7.1943 sank in position 53.36 N, 36.16 W.
5.7.1943	*Devis* (1)	Motorship	Whilst involved in the Invasion of Sicily was torpedoed and sunk by *U593* off Derna, Cape Dengut. Although no crew were lost, 52 out of her 289 Canadian troops perished due, mainly, to their heavy boots.

When founded in 1845 Lamport & Holt operated from offices at Fenwick Buildings, Fenwick Street, Liverpool. As the business grew they moved to larger premises in Drury Buildings, Water Street. (Above)

With control of Lamport & Holt Ltd passing to the Royal Mail Group in 1912 the firm moved to the Royal Liver Building on Liverpool's Waterfront.

In 1974 Lamport & Holt Line moved to Albion House, James Street, Liverpool, which was to remain its headquarters for the remainder of its existence. This building had originally been the headquarters of the White Star Line – Oceanic House. *(Photographs Courtesy Liverpool City Museum.)*

P.M. HEATON PUBLISHING

Paul Heaton was born at New Inn, Pontypool, in 1944 and was educated at Greenlawn Junior School in New Inn and the Wern Secondary School at Sebastopol. At fifteen he commenced employment, at first in a local store and then with a builders' merchant. A year later he was appointed as a Deck Cadet in the Merchant Navy, with the Lamport & Holt Line of Liverpool, and served in their vessels *Chatham, Constable* and *Romney* usually in the Brazil and River Plates trades. He joined the Monmouthshire Constabulary (now Gwent) in 1963, and served at Abergavenny, Cwmbran, Newport, the Traffic Department, the Motor Cycle Section, as the Press Liaison Officer, and for five years represented Inspectors for the whole of Wales nationally on the Joint Central Committee of the Police Federation. He was promoted to Sergeant in 1974 and Inspector in 1982. On his retirement he served as Market Inspector with the RSPCA for eight years and at the same time was Landlord of a Public House for three years.

He has always maintained an interest in maritime history and in transport generally, and for a period of ten years had numerous articles published in the magazine *Sea Breezes*. He has had the following books published:

Reardon Smith 1905-1980 (1980)
The Baron Glanely of St. Fagans and W.J. Tatem Ltd., with H.S. Appleyard (1980)
The 'Redbrook', A Deep-Sea Tramp (1981) four editions
The 'Usk' Ships (1982) two editions
The Abbey Line (1983)
Kaye, Son & Co. Ltd., with K. O'Donoghue (1983)
Reardon Smith Line (1984) two editions
The South American Saint Line (1985)
Welsh Blockade Runners in the Spanish Civil War (1985)
Lamport & Holt (1986) two editions
Tatems of Cardiff (1987)
Booth Line (1987)
Jack Billmeir, Merchant Shipowner (1989)
Welsh Shipping, Forgotten Fleets (1989)
The Gallant Ship 'Stephen Hopkins', with R.J. Witt (1990)
Palm Line, with Laurence Dunn (1994)
Not All Coppers Are ...! (1994)
Wynns – The First 100 Years for John Wynn (1995) three editions
Wynns – The Last 20 Years for John Wynn (1996)
L.C. Lewis, Heavy Haulage (1996)
Wynns Overseas first draft for John Wynn (1998)
The Wynns Fleet, 120 Years of Road Haulage (2003)
Lamport & Holt Line (2004)
Road Transport Gwent (2004)